MW00902933

Before You Go Any Further...
Please register your book now.

We have created an online addendum that contains live links to webpages, audio files and video – all designed to help you to see, hear and fully experience this exciting business case.

Social Media is changing rapidly and we want to ensure that you are kept up-to-date. Register your book right now so that you can you can get these materials.

Go to http://www.Barack20.com/addendum.html

If you have any questions, comments or concerns please contact us at info@barack20.com. We look forward to hearing from you.

"Whether you voted for Barack Obama or not, and whether you agree with his policies or not — I'd say you should agree that he did a masterful job using the Web to develop relationships and cement his candidacy.

In the 2004 election, everyone remarked how well Howard Dean leveraged the Web. Today Dean looks like a rank amateur compared to the level that President-elect Obama brought it to.

Lots of lessons to be learned. And I agree, those lessons translate well for small businesses because the underlying principles are timeless and involve human nature. And after all, business is ultimately about relationships."

– Anita Campbell, Editor – www.SmallBizTrends.com

"Social media was a key differentiator in a contest in which a virtual unknown won over a world audience and moved voters to act. That proves the power of listening and relationships more then anything anyone might say."

Liz Strauss, Founder SOBCon, www.successful-blog.com

"If you ever wanted a case study for social media return on investment you only have to look at the millions generated by Obama's social media team."

Chris Garrett, ProBlogger Co-Author – www.chrisg.com

"If anyone still doubts whether New Media Marketing is something they should take advantage of for their business, just look at Barack's win and ask yourself, can I afford NOT to use New Media to get the word out for my business, platform or campaign?"

~ Deborah Cole Micek, Founder of BLOGi360.com - http://TribalSeduction.com

"Social media being a new media, it is too early to look for many success stories. One exception however is the Barack Obama Campaign machinery that used the social media tools and best practices to create, engage and mobilize the community. Brent Leary and David Bullock have done a great job at Barack20.com to turn this success story into a case study that any business large or small can emulate themselves."

Shashi Bellamkonda, Network Solutions, www.shashi.name

"Excellent information, thanks for sharing. I am doing most of the things you mentioned, (blog, Twitter, Facebook, LinkedIn, etc) so that was great confirmation."

Barbara J. Faison - www.dontstress.net

"This info and President-Elect's use of social media gave me the kick I needed to do even more. I've taken my blog up 2 or 3 more notches which is giving me a very strong showing in Google's organic searches. I have 2 TV channels, SlideShare presentations that turn my articles into pictures, and a lot more. Thanks for the great work."

Peggy Duncan - www.suiteminute.com

"I discovered your site tonight and am so excited to learn about what you are sharing. President Obama's social media strategy influenced how I have developed and implemented my social media strategy and marketing plan as an author and entrepreneur. I will definitely visit your site on a regular basis to learn more about social media. Thanks for all you do."

Ananda Leeke - www.lovestroubadours.com

"I got a lot of very good information and tips on using social media to get people on my site and getting them involved. There are so many tools that I was unaware of and will be using. EXCELLENT info."

Norma Serrano - www.specialcelebrationgifts.com

Barack Obama's
Social Media Lessons for Business
with Interactive Online Companion

Brent Leary • David Bullock
Forward by Paul Greenberg

Put the Tools and Strategies to Work for Your
Business That Helped the Obama Campaign
Connect, Engage and Communicate with Millions.

Barack 2.0 – Barack Obama's Social Media Lessons for Business

"Barack 2.0: Barack Obama's Social Media Lessons for Business"
Published in arrangement with LuLu, Inc.,
and www.Barack20.com

PRINTING HISTORY
LuLu, Inc. - Global Market Distribution / 2008

For information address:
White Bullock Group, Inc.
1784 W. Northfield Blvd. Suite 162
Murfreesboro, TN 37129

Visit our website at
www.Barack20.com

ISBN: 978-0-578-00802-8

PRINTED IN THE UNITED STATES OF AMERICA

Acknowledgments

The rekindling of an old relationship started us on this exciting journey. There was no question we would have fun with the creation of this workbook. Our gratitude goes out to the many people involved in the development of *Barack 2.0 - Social Media Lessons for Business*.

Brent Leary and David Bullock would like to thank the following people for their contributions to this workbook:

- Paul Greenburg, President of Fifty-Six Group, http://the56group.typepad.com
- James Andrews, Vice President of Ketchum Interactive, Founder of http://www.TheKeyInfluencer.com
- Jascha Franklin-Hodge, co-founder Blue State Digital, http://www.BlueStateDigital.com

For promotion and permissions:

- Atlanta News Talk Radio 1160, http://www.newstalk1160.com
- Black Enterprise, Sonya A. Donaldson, donaldsons@blackenterprise.com
- ScribD, Jason Bentley, http://www.ScribD.com
- Twitter Counter, Boris Veldhuijzen van Zanten, http://www.twittercounter.com
- SmallBizTrends.com, Anita Campbell, Editor
- SOBCon, Liz Strauss, Founder, www.successful-blog.com
- *ProBlogger*, Chris Garrett, Co-Author, www.chrisg.com
- BLOGi360.com, Deborah Cole Micek, Founder, http://TribalSeduction.com

Special thanks to Laura Acord and Stephanie Michaud for their participation in the development of this publication and for their tireless support and endless words of encouragement.

Many thanks, also, to those who were kind enough to endorse the book and website.

Without the support of our families and friends, this book would just be a stack of typing paper, great ideas and spent dreams. We are reminded daily we are truly blessed.

Foreword

There is no doubt in anyone with a brain cell that part of the reason Barack Obama won the 2008 Presidential election was due to an extraordinary internet presence and a solid policy for engaging his potential constituents in ways that made them feel they were part of history.

What was even more astonishing is that they actually did help make history in more ways than one.

On the one hand, the more obvious way they participated in the creation of history was by giving money, volunteering to go door to door, doing inside calls for donations and get out the vote actions, participating in town meetings, creating the town meetings, driving themselves and others to and from rallies and all the other indispensable things that go into a successful campaign. Oh yeah, and they voted for Barack Obama too - either early, absentee or the usual way - on Election Day.

But what was truly historic in a different way was that this was the first time that a digital community was one of the prime movers of a successful election. Sure, Howard Dean used the internet in 2004, but that's exactly it. He "used" the internet. This wasn't a community, it was a tool. In the campaign of Barack Obama, the Internet housed the community that helped drive his victory. The tools - the social media like blogs, texting, podcasts, and other broadcasting tools; outreach programs aimed at external communities and social networks like Facebook, led to the record millions in donations and the enormous volunteer armies that did the sweat work day in and day out to make Barack Obama POTUS.

Ironically, what Barack Obama did was to use the community organizing principles he learned and applied so many years ago - things that were written about by Sol Alinsky and others back in the 1950s. That wasn't new. But how he communicated and acted on those principles was new - because the generations who worked for him communicated via the Internet in ways never seen before and that affected ALL institutions be they political, social, economic, leisurely and....business.

That's why, when Brent Leary, one half of the duo that produced this book, contacted me about writing the foreword I was immensely happy to do so.

First, it's a really exciting era that we've entered - and it's one that Brent and David understand really well. Since all institutions are impacted by the social changes that have gone on and the revolution in communications that triggered them. Business is going to be hit about the hardest as they've begun to already scramble to figure out how to use the lessons of change in how they interact with their now empowered customers who, because of success stories like Barack Obama's, are expecting so much more from all the institutions they engage with, including the businesses.

That's what makes Brent and David's book so timely and useful. They are taking their longstanding expertise and the fruits of the Barack 2.0 blog/site that they've had for so long and distilling it in a way that provides you with the lessons your business needs to know. That means they are translating how a successful candidate for the presidency of the United States did things that apply to your business, not just for your current generations of customers but for the future customers that you need to grow.

Thing is, this is pretty damned timely in a period where the economy doesn't look all that great. Because, as you'll see, some of the lessons to be learned are those that help when you don't have a lot of bucks to distribute on branding, and marketing, and even on building loyalty among your customers.

Other lessons learned are for better times, when you are looking to just blow the covers off your current business ROI and grow, grow, grow. Remember, President-elect Obama pulled in $55 million in a single month during the campaign. Hmmmmm...

The other thing? This book is actually enjoyable because Brent and David have this rapport that makes it easy for you to engage them in conversation - and that's how it feels as you get through it.

Okay, enough of me pontificating on how great this book is and what you might learn. Just go read it for yourself now. Go.

See ya.

Paul Greenberg

Author, CRM at the Speed of Light, 4th Edition

Table of Contents

Barack 2.0 Updates (continued)

Introduction

This book and its accompanying interactive online companion addendum make up the definitive reference on the use of social media, as it applies to small business. Brent Leary and David Bullock developed these collections of lessons over the course of 12 months. There are currently no restrictions on the use of procedures or principles, public or private. The images cannot be resold or distributed without license from those who hold the copyright.

> The interactive online companion can be located on the internet at
> http://www.Barack20.com/addendum.html

What is Barack 2.0?

We hope the lessons contained in this workbook will help you understand the impact a social media strategy can have on businesses of any size. This is not about politics. This workbook is about viewing Barack Obama's campaign use of Facebook, Twitter, YouTube and other sites from a business perspective. Democrats, Republicans and/or Independents can use these lessons alike. It's about understanding how we can use technology to meaningfully connect with people to build long-lasting relationships, turning clicks into customers, and using content to convert strangers into collaborators. These are the true lessons that we can take away from Barack Obama's improbable rise from obscurity to the presidency.

How Did Barack 2.0 Begin?

"I'll tell you something about Barack Obama that the media has not picked up on. He has got a very, very powerful presence on Facebook, on MySpace, on a lot of these sort of below the radar social networking sites on the internet." This quote, attributed to www.BlueMassGroup.com co-founder David Kravitz, appeared in a February 2007 New York Sun article entitled Obama's Facebook. (http://www.nysun.com/opinion/obamas-facebook/48560/)

This was just one month after Senator Obama announced his improbable candidacy for the presidency of the United States, and several months before Facebook opened its site up to the general public. By then, Obama already had over 250,000 fans on Facebook. Hillary Clinton, the overwhelming favorite to win the Democratic nomination, only had roughly 3,200.

The article captured David Bullock's attention, and led him to keep an eye on what Obama's campaign was doing with social media. Brent Leary had also become captivated with Obama's use of Web 2.0 tools and their impact on his campaign. When Brent shared with David the article he had written for Black Enterprise after Obama's stunning victory over Senator Clinton for the Democratic nomination in June, he was reminded of how prophetic David Kravitz was.

The fact that David and Brent were talking at all was pretty amazing, considering they hadn't seen or heard from each other in over 18 years, when they both were attending the University of Delaware. Just the month before in May 2008, they ran into each other at the Black Enterprise Entrepreneur's Conference. They both happened to be presenting at the Small Business Boot Camp – David on Internet Marketing and Brent on using technology to grow small businesses. What they observed from the attendees was a thirst for understanding how they could create a presence on the web that would allow them to reach the people looking for the products and services they provide. They were looking to understand how blogging, podcasting, video and social networks could help them compete in the marketplace.

With the huge excitement being generated by Obama's historic presidential bid, and interest in social media growing daily, David and Brent thought it would be interesting to analyze Obama's use of these technologies, not from a political perspective, but from the perspective of a businessperson looking to put together a social media strategy of their own.

They decided to turn their personal curiosity for Obama's social media moves into a webinar outlining some of the tools, strategies and methods used by his campaign to meaningfully engage millions of people. Being somewhat overwhelmed by the response they received by the small business community, they decided to create a blog/podcast that would allow them to dig a little deeper into different aspects of the social media strategy being implemented by the Obama campaign, which they began calling Barack 2.0. This led to the Barack20.com website and the Barack 2.0 Strategy Update podcast series.

Barack 2.0

Barack Obama's Social Media Lessons for Business

Put the tools and strategies to work for your business that helped the Obama campaign win friends and influence millions

The site picked up a loyal following and caught the attention of national media outlets. The interest in Barack 2.0 led to invitations to speak at industry conferences, professional organizations, and university MBA programs. Finally, after Obama's historic victory - and its description as the most successful Internet marketing campaign ever - it led to this workbook.

How to Use Barack 2.0

The tools and principles included in this workbook will serve to work for your business to win friends and influence millions. Social media is a blanket term used to describe any of several online platforms that utilize the technology of the internet to facilitate social interaction through written, visual, or audible communication.

Examples of social media methods include blogging, podcasts, forums, online press releases, and social networking platform sites like Facebook and Twitter. The use of social media as a marketing tool has quickly become prominent in the modern business world, and it can be an extremely effective way to promote products and services to a targeted audience. Websites function as a static billboard to promote your products, services, or ideas, but social media has created an opportunity for dynamic dialogue with your audience. The dialogue allows for interaction and personal connection. There is simply no other presentation of these principles with as much power and flexibility as Barack 2.0.

Social media marketing has several advantages over traditional marketing strategies.

Efficient - Unlike many traditional marketing methods, social media marketing provides an instant connection between you and your target audience. As soon as you create content and place the information up on the internet, it immediately becomes easily available to a large number of people. By contrast, television or radio commercials can take weeks to produce, billboards take time to print and install, and postcards and mailers can take several days to travel through the postal service.

Affordable - Social media marketing is extremely cost-effective when compared to other marketing methods. Many social networking platforms charge little or no fee to register, allowing you to utilize their services to locate and interact with your target audience without having to spend large amounts to do so. When compared to the cost of sending out flyers or postcards in the mail or shooting and airing a television commercial, social media is easily the more valuable option in terms of budget.

Effective - Social media allows your information to become available to millions of people through the internet. It can be used to reach very specific niches, ensuring that your marketing is attracting the attention of people who will be interested in what you have to say. Listing your blog on directory websites allows people to find it by searching for specific subjects or causes. Social networking platforms allow you to join or create groups, inviting like-minded individuals to share dialogue with you about your products, services, or ideas. Achieving top rankings on search engines can be aided by building relationships through various forms of social media to encourage the promotion of your site, company or organization to readers who would otherwise be unaware of its existence.

Interactive - Unlike most traditional marketing strategies, social media allows you to begin a conversation with your audience, creating a dialogue. Encouraging your audience to provide feedback and express their ideas and suggestions about your business. Customers who have taken the time to build a personal connection with you and/or your business feel as though you care about their opinions, feelings and feedback. They are more likely to return to you when they need your services again. For organizations trying to promote an idea or cause, social media allows you to have discussions with people, informing them about your cause and potentially changing minds with an interactive dialogue.

The key elements in achieving success through social media marketing are an open mind and a considerable amount of patience. It often takes several months for these tools to really provide tangible results. Traditional measurements of Return on Investment (ROI) do not always apply to the world of web marketing. However, internet marketing continues to be one of the least expensive and most effective ways to promote your business.

Unfortunately, many companies and organizations leap into social media marketing without the knowledge or experience of how to use it properly. The most common mistakes include using blogs solely to promote products or services, providing inaccurate or uninteresting content, scraping content from other sites, and failing to engage in honest dialogue with their audiences. Getting started on the right foot is essential in executing a successful social media marketing campaign. Some of the beginning strategies will include setting up blogs, web pages and social networking profiles. Your current site(s) will need to be optimized for social media interaction.

Congratulations on taking the first step in your journey to success. *Barack 2.0: Barack Obama's Social Media Lessons for Business* will be essential in educating yourself on how to successfully utilize these platforms to ensure the best possible results for your business or organization.

There are a few tools and principles that everyone will use, several others that most will use, and many more that only few will use. The most advanced users may even combine programs and tools to create new functionality specific to their needs, and we will offer some guidance for them as well.

These tools will be presented in the same order as they were identified in the Barack Obama 2008 campaign. This book is a written representation of the interaction on the www.Barack20.com website. Therefore, as you might guess, there are several online references. These references are easily identified with the icons below and can be accessed via the interactive online companion.

 Audio Available Online

 Addendum Reference

 Transcription – Verbatim Transcription of Barack 2.0 Updates

 Recommended Websites

Overview

By: Brent Leary and David Bullock

Barack Obama Social Media Lessons for Business

Posted by Brent | Wednesday 30 July 2008 9:34 pm

In many ways, the challenges Barack Obama's presidential campaign faced are representative of the obstacles we run into every day as small business owners and entrepreneurs. It may not appear as if this is the case, as we see him on television, on the cover of national publications and in photographs with world leaders. However, that wasn't always the case, as many of us had never heard of him just four years ago. In addition, even when he announced his candidacy, political insiders...or outsiders for that matter still didn't take him seriously.

Somehow, he and his campaign went from these inauspicious beginnings to winning (presumably) his party's nomination for the presidency. How did he do it? There are various reasons for the way things have turned out to date. One area that continues to have a significant (and still growing) impact on the outcome is social media. The Obama campaign has leveraged social media tools and strategies to:

- Organize and energize millions of people at the grass roots level

- Engage people who have not participated in the political process to be active members

- Raise hundreds of millions of dollars - much of it coming from ordinary citizens

The Obama campaign has fully utilized social media to change the way political campaigns are managed. There are many lessons small business people can learn from studying his campaign. Just as Obama has used tools like Twitter, Facebook and YouTube to "win friends and influence people," small business people can do so as well. Finding enough new customers efficiently is one of the leading challenges small businesses face.

We may never have 1M fans on Facebook, or 50K followers on Twitter. We can only dream about raising hundreds of millions of dollars through our blogs and websites. Lucky for us, we don't need to. We're not running for president, we're running to be competitive and profitable.

The focus of this site is on helping small businesses, startups and entrepreneurs learn from the moves the Obama campaign made with respect to social media. For us, this is not about politics - it's about business.

In fact, below is our "official statement" so you know exactly where we stand on this:

We have no affiliation to Barack Obama, or his campaign to be the next President of the United States of America. Our focus is solely on how the Obama campaign used social media to engage people at the grass roots level in order to win millions of votes and break political fundraising records. We do not talk about political views or take political positions. We look at the role social media played in his campaign, the tools and strategies they deployed, and the lessons small businesses can put to work for themselves.

We hope that helps set the stage for everything you see on the site going forward. We look to you to make sure we stay on point with our objectives.

We look forward to sharing with you some of the things we feel will help you get a better understanding for how social media can impact your business. Whether it is a blog post, a webinar, e-book or other form of digital content, the objective will always be to help you benefit from the social media lessons Barack Obama's campaign is putting together for us all.

Brent Leary and David Bullock

Webinar

Barack Obama's
Social Media Lessons for Business

July 9th, 2008

A few weeks back David Bullock and I had a conversation/webinar highlighting some of the reasons we felt small business people would benefit from taking a closer look at the Obama campaign's approach to social media. We recorded it for your on-demand viewing:

Barack 2.0 Webinar - Part 1 - http://barack20.com/downloads/Video%201

Barack 2.0 Webinar - Part 2 - http://barack20.com/downloads/Video%202

To download an electronic copy of the transcript with enabled internet links, please visit: http://barack20.com/downloads/Transcript1_Barack20_Webinar_1

We've also put together an enhanced transcript of the webinar below, complete with screenshots and links to the sites we discussed during the conversation:

Barack 2.0 Webinar
Enhanced Transcript and Resource Guide

Brent Leary: My name is Brent Leary. I have a company called CRM Essentials and I do some writing for Inc. Magazine and Black Enterprise. I am joined today with a friend that I hadn't seen in about nineteen years. We'll explain that a little bit. David Bullock, CEO of White Bullock Group, Inc. and online business development expert, David, thanks for joining me man.

David Bullock: No problem, glad to be here, Sir.

Brent Leary: As I said, we hadn't seen each other in about nineteen years. We actually went to the University of Delaware together and three months ago or so, we just so happened to both be speaking at the same event, the Black Enterprise Entrepreneurs Conference. David was doing an excellent presentation on internet marketing.

David Bullock: Exactly, we went over the ins and outs of getting a business online. It was very interesting because I was doing the internet marketing side and then right after my presentation you did your piece on CRM services, the internet and social media. Immediately we realized we were in the same space and didn't even know it.

Brent Leary: That was really what set us on this path of the Barack Obama 2.0 because of the response that we saw from the group when we both did our presentations. There was just a lot of energy and a lot of excitement and there were many questions. As I mentioned a little bit before, I write for Black Enterprise and I did an article called "Barack Obama: Social Media Lessons for Business." David and I talked about it and we thought it would be a great, sort of like a case study for small businesses to go over some of the things that he used in order to get to where he is today from near obscurity, as little as four years ago. We just want to take you through a couple of points. If you have any questions, we'd love to hear them. David let's go ahead and get this started.

David Bullock: Okay, here we go.

Brent Leary: Small business, we are all trying to figure out a couple of things and it's all centered around how do we attract new business and it's a really simple concept here. People like buying from people they like. Just think about that in terms of when we do our own buying for things on a personal level. I find it much easier to buy from somebody who is knowledgeable about their service, friendly, and easy to talk to. It makes me want to give up my money a little easier, how about you David?

Sales & Marketing Challenges

- **The Problem**

- **Average Business has 7% Awareness**

- **90%+ of Market Not Ready to Buy**

- **Awareness = 6-7 Touches Per Year**

- **80% of New Sales Take 8-15 Contacts to Gain Interest**

- **Avg. Salesperson Abandons After 1-2 Calls**

- **50% of All Leads Buy – in 6-18 Months**

- **Result: Huge Numbers of Missed Opportunities**

Source: Cargill Consulting Group, Inc., Griffin Consulting Group, Sales & Marketing Mgmt Magazine, Harvard Business Review, Dartnell Institute

David Bullock: Exactly, when the internet first came about people started hiding behind computers. Meaning, they became faceless, but now you are seeing a very significant juxtaposition within the marketplace on how people use the online media and it's becoming a lot more relationship oriented. We are finally getting back to where we are dealing with people and talking to people and actually developing relationships online.

Brent Leary: If you take that online message, we do it great face to face. All small business people are excellent face to face because we know how to talk to people; we know we are trying to earn their business. It's hard to do that online, but it's important to try to realize or recognize that we can get people to like us face to face. We can get them to trust us face to face but the trick is how we get folks to like us and trust us when they don't know us. They don't know we exist. They could be halfway around the world and still needing our product and services and they need to find a way to get to us.   Of course, we are small business people and we have limited means. It's critical to try to figure out how we can leverage the web and things like social media. We'll talk about that in a bit. But how we can use the web to reach the people who can use what we have right away and that's the biggest challenge I see. David, please feel free to help me out because we all go to these trade shows and we all do out networking events and we do meet people; it looks like they may be a good fit for us, but chances are we are not walking out with a check right after meeting them.

David Bullock: Exactly.

Brent Leary: It's really important to find ways to keep in touch with people when you meet them face to face, or the people who are searching for good products or service information on the web. They may come across you on a search, but what's going to keep them engaged with you until the point where they are ready to do business?

Our challenge as small business people is being found, and it's also captivating the people once they find us. To keep them around long enough so that when they do make that decision to buy we're at the forefront of their mind and they will reach out to us when they are ready to do something.   Of all of the examples David, we've talked about this a lot; we need real examples for this because small business people are still on the fence about this. Are you picking that up as well?

David Bullock: Definitely. Right now, the web is still a very intimidating place. There is still the idea that you have to go to websites, it is highly technical, and you have to figure out how to get into the search engines that's highly technical. There is still a lot, I would almost say misinformation, information, which is old. There is such a renaissance of new information, new ways that the internet is actually moving, new ways in which the search engines are working and better yet how people are using the internet.

That brings us into the conversation of Web 2.0, we've heard the buzz word, Web 2.0, and you hear about these situations where people are developing these applications and they're selling them out for millions sometimes hundreds of millions of dollars to say one of the big search engines or any of the large corporate entities.

The question now becomes how can you, as a small business owner, not only first understand what Web 2.0 is and better yet how to use it, what to use and how to use it most effectively. If you can hold that question in mind as we go through this case study and this is a real live case study, you have seen this play out on your television and in the news within the last several months. Barack Obama, Yes we can. Let's look at this: He's a black guy with a funny name, in fact a notorious middle name...

Barack Obama

A Black guy...
With a funny name...
And that notorious middle name...
Having serious pastor problems...
What is that he is wearing?
Wants to be the next POTUS?

Say What?

Brent Leary: We know what it rhymes with, right?

David Bullock: Right, we know what it rhymes with. At one point, you looked at the media and you saw that he had some very significant PR issues with one of the people that he was associated with, his pastor. You have a picture of him wearing this type of outfit and now he wants to be the President of the United States. Come on!

The Impossible Market

Brent Leary: Yeah, who would have thought four years ago and say what, because that's what we were all thinking, right? I mean, how could he do this?

David Bullock: Exactly.

Brent Leary: Let's see what he did do. He's raised 300 million dollars; actually, this slide is outdated. He raised 300 million dollars, most of it, the chunk of it over the web and in small amounts from ordinary people. I like putting out that he won in contests like in Iowa, Montana, and North Dakota where David, I don't know about you but I don't have any family out there, do you?

David Bullock: No kin folk in those parts that I know of. How's that...

Brent Leary: None that either of us knows of. He was able to go from somebody who we didn't know about four years ago. I believe when he first announced his campaign for presidency about eighteen/nineteen months ago nobody really gave him a second thought and look what he's done so far. It is truly amazing and one of the cool things about it is, just two days ago, there was an article on how one of the Facebook co-founders actually took a leave from Facebook to go and work on the Obama Campaign and sort of head up the social media efforts. There's a quote in there from Barack Obama himself that said that social media had a big role in getting him to where he is today.

David Bullock: Right, he recognizes that. Let's reframe this. Barack Obama, let's look at him as the business owner and he is going into a market, an impossible market against the incumbent, the power couple in the United States. The guy has been there in office. His spouse is a Senator, so he's not only battling against a business that is just like him, he's already behind the eight ball and she has help.

Try to frame Barack Obama as the business owner, coming into an impossible market, trying to sell product. If you can frame this presentation that we are going to do from here on out that way you are going to start seeing some very significant analogies. What we'd like you to do is see how you can use that in your markets because I doubt if they are as impossible or as huge as this market that we are looking at now.

The Blogging Platforms

Brent Leary: Absolutely.   Let's step through a couple of things here, I think the easiest one that pretty much... I should not say that. I was at a conference not too long ago speaking about this and there's about forty people in the room and I asked how many of you blog and outside of the presenters, no hands went up.

I figure it is important to say, first and foremost, Barack has a blog and he uses it effectively. It's not just him and we are going to take a quick look at the slide of it but he puts out relevant information. It doesn't have to be earth shattering but when you think about blogging, it's a way for you to open the lines of communication. Not use one-way communication but a full conversation and as small business people trying to figure out the web, that's what we want, we want to engage people in a conversation that will keep them involved with us up until a point where they are ready to do a deal.

 See Addendum – Figure Web1.1

David Bullock: Exactly and one of the things we like to point out about a blog is a blog looks like a website but there's some things that are going on in the back of a blog that makes the search engines love it. A search engine comes by and sees a blog or a blogging platform and it just devours the blogging platform and says this is good relevant information that is up to date. The internet is changing. The actual infrastructure is changing. You had to be out there forever, you had to have ten thousand pages to now they are just like look give us good information and keep it coming to us and we will be back everyday to see what you are talking about.   As a business owner that puts you out in front of the people that you want to be in front of.

Brent Leary: One of the things that we also want to point out is that everything that we touch on here is definitely within reason for any small business to do. Just for an example, I've got a screen up here for www.Blogger.com. Blogger is a really good tool. A free tool that small business people can use to get a blog set up, you see what it says on the screen. Three easy steps it take a couple of minutes probably but you can get started with these things quickly. There are other blogging tools and I use one call TypePad. David I think you use WordPress.

David Bullock: I use WordPress, correct.

Social Media Platforms

Brent Leary: WordPress, so there are a number of tools and most of them are very easy to use. We just wanted to point out this one because hey, it's free and you can get started with it rather quickly. Barack blogs and he also is on Facebook. If you don't have an account or profile on Facebook it's really time to consider it, because there are seventy or eighty million people on Facebook.

David Bullock: That's right, a lot of folks.

Brent Leary: The fastest growing demographic is 35 and over. These are people who are really more business oriented or at least in addition to being more personal with the profile, but they have a business side to them and so it's really important to understand that Facebook is not for kids as a matter of fact, as we look at this page here, this is Barack Obama's Facebook page.

    See Addendum – Figure Web1.2

    To Visit Barack Obama's Facebook page - http://www.facebook.com/barackobama?ref=s

You can see under supporters, there are over a million supporters. It would be great to have that kind of support, but David, as small business people, we don't really need a million people.

David Bullock: No, you need to get the attention of the people who want, need and can afford your product and services. Again, look at this.   We are showing you an example of someone who is on television, on the radio, moving all around and he's attracting attention. As a business owner, you have to be in position to get the attention. If there are seventy million people on Facebook, guess what. There is a stream of possibilities there. What you want to do is get in front of it and if they are over at Facebook, you need to be there too.   The thing is set up for teenagers. If you can type and you can send an email, you can be on Facebook and you can use Facebook effectively. There are some ins and outs about doing it effectively because this is not advertisement. You are not necessarily promoting. It's not the way that you would run into someone at a networking event and promote yourself. This is actually building relationships, which is a completely different skill set that a lot of us need to learn how to do that online. But it's the best way to get business.

Brent Leary: Absolutely. It's just another tool in the tool chest. Barack also has a YouTube channel and you are familiar with some of the videos that have come out, either directly from Obama or from the millions of people that have been engaged with him and are following him. It's a really great mechanism, to get people to reach out to you to start a conversation. We are taking a quick look at Barack Obama's YouTube channel and we're going to talk a lot about video in a few minutes but we wanted to point this out. Once again, YouTube channel – free. Something that all you need is what? A webcam, David? You can get started as easily as that.

 See Addendum – Figure Web 1.3

 To Visit Barack Obama's YouTube Channel - http://youtube.com/user/barackobamadotcom

David Bullock: Exactly, it doesn't take very much now. The technology exists; the venues for distribution are out there for you. They are available and being highly promoted, it's time for you to leverage what's already there. YouTube is one of at least I think twenty some odd video outlets available in the marketplace right now.

Brent Leary: Absolutely, and Uncle Barack has widgets too David.

David Bullock: Mmhmm

Brent Leary: I just love that, widgets are just snippets of code that you can just cut and paste onto your website webpage that gives you fresh updated content. It was impressive how Barack set up a number of widgets, so as you can see he has a widget for latest video. Anytime a video gets loaded up to his YouTube channel, it has a little widget that if you put that on your site, it updates your site automatically without you having to do anything. If there are some latest news developments, he has a latest new widget. Actually, he has many widgets. Once again, widgets are viral David and that is really something that will help small businesses get the word out.

David Bullock: Let me point some things out here. Barack Obama has 120 widgets.

Brent Leary: Wow.

 See Addendum – Figure Web 1.4

David Bullock: He has many little emissaries out in the marketplace speaking and talking to people when he's asleep. That's a dream of most marketers. If you notice, the viral element here is very pronounced. Look at that, 4100 installs of the latest video. 3,500+ installs of the latest news, which means that all he did was create it and people were so interested in what he was doing that they wanted to put his information on their outlets, their blogs, websites, Facebook pages.

Again, this is the idea that if you have information that people want to share, it goes out there. Imagine having 4100 sales people working for your business tirelessly, day in and day out while you're doing something else. That's really what you have and again I want to make the analogy for what Barack is doing and how that really correlates to real physical business.

Brent Leary: Absolutely and we're going to touch on Twitter a lot later on, but Twitter is another tool that Barack has used effectively. This is what drove me to write the article. For those who aren't familiar, Twitter is a micro blogging tool so instead of doing a full blown 700 word blog. You can use Twitter to just shoot out a short sentence and little update on what's going on in your industry or maybe if you have a new blog post or just to alert people. Twitter allows folks to follow you and get updates on you, it can be on their cell phone their mobile device or the web or probably a thousand different kinds of Twitter tools that are out there. There are over a million people on Twitter and here we are looking at Barack Obama's Twitter page and David, the number that stands out to many people is that 41,000 people follow him.

 See Addendum – Figure Web 1.5

David Bullock: Exactly, so you have 41,000 people following Barack Obama. That means that any time that he has a thought, anything that he tweets out there on this particular platform, it goes out to 41,000 people. Now granted, if you have a hundred, two hundred, three hundred a thousand people following you and you said hey I found a new resource that would be helpful to them. You become the authority within the marketplace.

As an authority in the marketplace, you can command more income and it becomes easier to sell because you are not selling, people already know, like and trust you. You have been giving them good information. So if you look here that 41,000 people are following him but look at the other number here. He has followers at 39,000 and he is following 41,000. He has actually done something, which is like a professional courtesy. "Hey if you are going to follow me, I'm going to follow you" and look at his updates. He's doesn't just have an account and he's not working it. At this time when we took this screen shot there were 136 updates. He has actually participated in the community, which is very important in this new Web 2.0 space.

Using Podcasts

Brent Leary: We are going to contrast that with somebody else who is using Twitter or at least used Twitter to compare how it worked out for both of those folks. However, one of the things close to my heart is podcasting. He has podcasts and, his podcasts are loaded up in iTunes and anybody who is interested or likes music, there are millions of people walking around with these things. You cannot only buy music but you can download podcasts free. iTunes is actually the #1 Podcast directory on the web and 75% of all podcasts actually come or are downloaded from iTunes.

Podcasting can be as easy as attaching a microphone to your laptop and giving your take on what's going on in the industry. Creating that easy MP3 file, loading it up to the web and it's another way for people to take in information. David, I like taking in information audibly, maybe from when I am on the treadmill or if I am waiting in the airport and I think, a lot more people are getting into that.

 See Addendum – Figure Web 1.6

David Bullock: There's an underlying piece here. When you put a podcast out there into the marketplace and someone is able to download it into their MP3 player, they can detach from their computer. They don't have to be at the computer to hear your message which means you can actually have a one on one conversation with them while they are driving to work or while they are on the treadmill.

Podcasting gives a new level of freedom for someone to take and consume your information and with video podcasting with the MP3 players, which also allow video to be played on there. Now you can have a full interface, meaning full sight and sound right in the palm of someone's hand away from the computer, in their spare time while they are relaxing. Take a look at the nuance here. They have taken the time to download your material and they have taken the time to consume it, which means that they are reaching for you. All you did was put it out there for them to consume.

Brent Leary: Enhanced podcasts are really excellent because like you said, it's not just hearing; now they're seeing. It could be PowerPoint slides that you are talking about what's going in your industry or your expertise and it adds another dimension to the experience of them taking in information. You are almost able to captivate them and that's exactly what small businesses want to do. You need to create content that will captivate people because there is so much information out there, we are trying to win the minds and hearts of people who we want to do business with, and there are many other people that are trying to do the same. It's really important to find the right tools and the right format that are going to entice the people to take in the information and build that dialogue with you. Barack has done a great job with that.

> ## Podcast
>
> A new word for a recent technology. Prior to 2004, the word podcast was unknown.
>
> In 2008, Oxford English Dictionary announced the addition of the words podcasting, podcast, podcaster and pod-casted to the OED.
>
> Another great example of how the internet and its technology is changing our world and our vocabulary.

David Bullock: Right. The whole idea of podcasting, if you are a person who says that "I have a face for radio, and I don't want my face out there" you use your voice and overlay a PowerPoint on top of your voice. Just as well, you do a one-on-one presentation with your prospect or your visitor and your face is not there.

Brent Leary: It's really easy to get started.   Check out www.BlogTalkRadio.com.

  See Addendum – Figure Web 1.7

It's a great service for those who aren't like me who have geeked out completely on all sorts of audio equipment. I'm not even going to say how much I have spent, but you don't have to spend a dime to go to www.BlogTalkRadio.com. You can use their service and have your own radio show up and running in no time. Then it's a great way to interview experts in the field and raise your credibility and if you can get a conversation with a bonafide expert and your having a conversation with them and you can put that out on the web, you just raised your credibility because you're there going one-on-one right with an expert. That is a great way to build your credibility and an inexpensive one too.

David Bullock: Exactly, it's a matter of borrowing the identity of the expert and it just rubs off. They say birds of a feather flock together and you're known by the company that you keep. If you interview up and get those industry experts in an intelligent conversation and giving good content, It's evergreen. Meaning, you could have that conversation one time and it could play for years and continue to get you traffic and continue to get you credibility within the marketplace.

Brent Leary: We went through a number at a very high level of the tools that the Obama campaign used to really spread the word out, engage people, and of course raise $300MM, we can't forget that.

David Bullock: Exactly.

Brent Leary: We're going to focus in on two of them specifically. We are going to talk a little bit more about the video components and we are going to talk a little bit about YouTube and we're also going to talk about Twitter. I will point out before we get there that LinkedIn is definitely a tool that many small businesses have bought into as a great social network for a professional and business minded people.

One of the cool things that Obama's campaign did right at the beginning when LinkedIn started doing the LinkedIn answers, which was probably about seven or eight months ago, maybe even longer than that. Who was the first person that they went to, to use that utility? It was Barack Obama and the question he posed to the LinkedIn crowd was "What are you looking for in your next president?" Over a thousand replies to the question.

It's a great way to engage people to start a conversation. FriendFeed is a brand new one comparatively speaking but it is catching a lot of steam, so you'll want to check out www.FriendFeed.com. We don't have time to really focus on those right now but I just wanted to point those out. David, I know that you were all over this video the YouTube with Barack Obama.

Video Components

   See Addendum – Figure Web 1.8

David Bullock: Let's not just look at it. We want to dissect it and see what's really going on here on this page. First of all, it's YouTube and as you can see, this is David S. Bullock. I have an account on YouTube. I am not just waving my arms here and saying go do this, no I am using these tools on a day-to-day basis.   YouTube was bought by Google. We know that Google is the 800 pound gorilla in the marketplace as far as search is concerned. You know that if they've bought it, they are using it within their search components.

Let's look at some things here. If you look at the top on the right hand side, it says that he joined a year ago, but he has 1145 videos. That is a lot of video footage.   This is a three-minute long video we have here. This is not an hour, it's not a half hour - it's less then five minutes. Anyone can develop video clips and if they are engaging and tell a message and they have a call to action. He has 1000 little salesmen out there speaking his message in the marketplace and the possibility of that happening every day. Let's look at this one video, 1,205,023. That's 1.2

million views of this one video. This is not counting the other 1144 videos, this is just one of his videos. Notice, he has comments 4,233 comments.

Brent Leary: That's the number that got me. That means that they are engaged with this.

David Bullock: Right and they are talking about it and because they are talking about it this video gets played and it gets on the front page of YouTube as the most viewed, most commented. Notice, he spoke my plan for 2008 one time. Filmed it one time and it's been talking for him since January 16, 2007. It's still talking for him now.

Brent Leary: What's really good about this is this is not a big major production; this is just him sitting in front of a camera in a chair.   I think we can probably do that as well Dave, the small business person?

David Bullock: Exactly, you get the video camera; most of us have video footage. Most of us have things that we've already done in or around our business, that you can put a front and a back on, put it up on YouTube, start promoting it. One thing that I would also like to point out here, which I find very interesting, notice, it says "more from www.BarackObama.com." He is giving you the website to go to for more information.

Brent Leary: Yes, that's what is key. We small business people, we want to move these people to act. That means go to a place on the web where we want to engage them even further.

David Bullock: Exactly.   Look at the other viral components here. If you look right below where it says rate, it says share. Okay, as soon as you say "share" - boom. MySpace sends this video to a friend, puts it on Facebook and other share options.   Which means, the viral, the sharability of this video or your video is already built into the YouTube platform. That's how he is able to get so many views. Someone says, hey listen to what Barack is saying and Boom. If you have good information which is out there and it's worthy to be shared, it will be shared and that's what leads to the viral appeal.

    See Addendum – Figure Web 1.9

Now, we move on to www.blip.tv, which is another video situation, which is available online.

This is Oprah Winfrey for Barack Obama. He is engaged with the celebrities that have a broad appeal within the marketplace. This video, look at the logo, CNN, right there, so you have Oprah Winfrey, with Barack Obama and you have the CNN logo, right there on the video.

Notice the credibility which is just in the one picture that we have here. Then, Oprah goes on and speaks for Barack Obama. People can see this video over and over and over again. They can share the video. Notice they are on the right hand side, share, and email. The viral component is available here. This is not YouTube this is blip.tv. You will notice that all of the video venues all of the vendors out there have this shareability factor built right in. When you put something out there, it is sharable.   So there it is.

David Bullock: I just noticed something else. Notice that you have Oprah Winfrey, Barack Obama and Hillary Clinton. Notice that Barack Obama and Hillary Clinton, who holds identity in the marketplace, or was holding or still is holding identity and Oprah Winfrey. We have all this stuff happening just because he is out there just this way.

Brent Leary: Absolutely and we are going to quickly go past Obama. This is really what got people all going with Barack on YouTube was this Obama Girl who was not affiliated with him at all.

    See Addendum – Figure Web 1.10

David Bullock: Notice the number of views, 8.9 million views. Whether you like it or not, she created buzz in the marketplace for him.

Brent Leary: Yes

David Bullock: Look at her number of videos, 115 videos. She has launched a completely new career based on linking herself with an identity that was moving in the marketplace, Senator Obama.   Again, as a business owner it's a video outlet.   How long is this thing? It is three minutes and 19 seconds.

Brent Leary: The other thing that I couldn't get in the snapshot - 42,000 comments. Just so we level it out a little bit because we know that Obama is in a stratosphere and we are looking at the tools and strategies that he used. I just came across this gentleman here. He calls himself the SEO rapper. First of all, how audacious is that, somebody talking about search engine optimization and putting it to rap.   Well, guess what folks and I highlight it in those circles, now he is over 300,000 views of this video and over 520 comments and I think around 1400 ratings and his average rating 4.5 on a number of 1500 votes. This is a guy that nobody knows about. The video was only added in March. This is a guy who was smart enough to think outside of the box and say, okay, I want to show my SEO skills, but I need to do it in a way that's going to attract attention. He came up with an interesting rap around search engine optimizations.   He has the channel. He has a number of videos, as David was pointing out.   Look at some of the others, although this is the number one video by way of views. He's got one that's almost 30,000 views and another that is 48,000 views. It's really interesting if you can use these technologies and think out of the box how many people you can reach.

> **YouTube**
> - Age Range 18--52
> - Equal male to female
> - All Geographies
> - Hundreds of Millions of Videos Are Viewed Daily
> - Hundreds of Thousands or Videos are Uploaded Daily
> - Every Minute 10 Hours of Video is Uploaded to YouTube
> http://www.youtube.com/t/fact_sheet

    See Addendum – Figure Web 1.11

David Bullock: Because of the attention that he has gotten, his video has gone viral and I've been in groups on the internet marketing side. They are inviting him to come perform and or be a paid speaker at some of the events.

Brent Leary: Yes

David Bullock: Once you start getting attention, people want you around. They want you to be there to share your expertise.   His expertise is understood to be Search Engine Optimization, conversion, Adwords, how to advertise online and he just put it into a different format, which is easily consumable, brought attention. He may have a whole other career starting to build because he just went ahead and put a three minute and twenty-two second video on YouTube.

Brent Leary: I will say this; he is not going to be standing on a Mount Rushmore of rap. He is no Rakim. He is no Biggie (Smalls), although he sort of looks like Biggie right there. The point is you don't have to be. You just need to give yourself time to think creatively about how you can engage people on the web, how do you reach them. That is the message here. As a matter of fact, I just did an article for www.SmallBizTrends.com. It's on their home page right now and I feature this guy because this guy committed in an audacious online act that needed to be highlighted. If you do these kinds of things, somebody is going to highlight you too. That is one of the important things that we wanted to point out.   Let's get into Twitter. Twitter is a monster.

 To read Brent's article visit –
http://www.smallbiztrends.com/2008/07/give-away-content-act-audacious.html/

David Bullock: Yeah.

The Twitter Monster

Brent Leary: David and I were just talking about that before we got on the call. There are about 1001 tools out there that are helping people use Twitter in the fashion that makes it convenient for them. Here is a snapshot of a site called Twitterholic.

 Visit Twitterholic here: http://twitterholic.com/

 See Addendum – Figure Web 1.12

It tracks the most followed people on Twitter and once again, our man Barack is coming in at number three. What's really interesting - let's side step Barack for a second. Has anybody heard of Leo Laporte? I barely heard of him a few months ago because he does an online radio show, but I never knew this guy five months ago, but look at how many people are following him.

David Bullock: Exactly and notice that Twitterholic is a gauge for attention in the marketplace. If you have 40,000 people waiting for you to say something, then you say something or recommend something; the odds are that some small percent of those people may just want to engage you in business.

Brent Leary: The point is, you have an audience, forty thousand people and as you said, you could type just I'm having salad today for lunch, hit a submit button and that thing goes out to 40,000 people on their mobile devices. There is a service called at OutTwit, so if you are a big Outlook user, there's an add-on for Twitter so you can get your tweets right from within Outlook. There are a number of ways people are being reached with Twitter and it's so easy to reach somebody. Typing a little thing and hit submit and it goes everywhere.

To visit OutTwit go to – http://www.techhit.com/OutTwit/

David Bullock: I did a tweet this morning and I found a new resource. I said, "Good morning I found this new resource, it's like this," pushed the button boom, the tweet went out to my followers and immediately I started getting emails.

Brent Leary: Man, thanks Dave, Great resources.

About

Name Barack Obama
Location Chicago, IL
Web http://www.barack...

Stats

Following	46,252
Followers	44,596
Favorites	0
Updates	147

David Bullock: Didn't sell them anything, but notice that I am building trust as we move along and that's why you use that particular platform. These two panels are on the side of the Twitter accounts. We want to point some things out to you. On the left, obviously, we have Barack Obama's history stat and then you have Hillary Clinton's stats. Notice, how many people are in the Barack Obama following when we grabbed this, 46,000 people. How many are Mrs. Hillary Clinton following, zero. There's no two way conversation going on here. It's just going out. It's like you follow me, but I don't care really about what you're doing. I'm not following you. The numbers show zero.

Notice here, he's following and he's got followers and he's updating at about the same rate. But there was something very interesting going on. If you go out online, you'll find out that bloggers were blogging about the fact that Barack Obama was following them. It caused an excitement in the marketplace that people were willing to talk about.

Again, you have to understand something, the search engines are one level of traffic. Search will start at the search engines but as soon as you leave the search engine and you start entering into the blogs and the websites and the links in between blogs and websites, there's a whole mountain of traffic there that you will never see unless you are in it. When the bloggers started saying Barack Obama's following me. They actually started linking back... he's following me too, he's following me, he's following me too. You have a million sites that are saying that Barack Obama is following me. That gets his name out there.

About

Name Hillary Clinton
Web http://hillarycli...
Bio
http://hillaryclinton.com/about/

Stats

Following	0
Followers	4,164
Favorites	0
Updates	175

block hillaryclinton

Brent Leary: Many sites are saying Hillary Clinton isn't following anyone.

David Bullock: Right

Brent Leary: That was the contrast that I drew, that it was great to see how many people were following them. The real telling statistic was the difference between their strategies, the Obama strategy of saying, hey look, we want to have a conversation. We may not look at all your tweets. We may not reply to all your tweets, but we're going to give you the courtesy of at least following your tweets.

David Bullock: Exactly.

Brent Leary: Whereas, the Clinton campaign took a completely and very different tact and said people I don't want to hear from you. I just want you to hear me and that is totally against what goes on in a Web 2.0 world. That is the key here. You want to use this to create a conversation and engage people and what you see is more people followed Barack because he followed more people.

David Bullock: It's a 10X difference, not a couple percentage points, ten times. Look at the amount of work involved here. The amount of work within the Twitter environment is the number of updates. He has 10X more people and he actually did less work with 147 updates against 175 updates. Hmmm, look at that.

Brent Leary: That's about, what, 15-20% less work?

David Bullock: Exactly.

Brent Leary: That's something to really take a note on. The Twitter platform is free and it is available, all Senator Obama did was use it effectively.

Brent Leary: Yes, absolutely. Folks, the key with Twitter, you see there's a lot of conversations going on in Twitter. You need to be hip to what's going on, what's being said in Twitter. We are all very familiar with Google and we all do our Google search and I hope you have your Google alerts set up on your name and your company name so that anything that comes out on a web page or a blog, you can at least know what is going on when your name is referenced. Well, guess what, your names are going to be referenced in these little tweets that are going on in Twitter.

Google Search

There's a tool that you need to know about that's called Summize. If you go to www.Summize.com (now www.Search.Twitter.com), it's similar to a Google search that happens within Twitter. If you want to see what is being said between all those millions of Twitter conversations? You put your name in and you start to see who's talking about you in Twitter and how important is that? It's incredibly important.

David Bullock: It's huge. To be able what people are saying about you? In this particular case, Senator Obama, let's gauge and get a pulse of the marketplace. Let's see what they are saying about me, how are we doing? That really is a survey, but it's a survey without you asking any questions. You're just dipping into the conversation. You're listening in. Let's look at this from a business standpoint. To go into the marketplace and find out what your market is talking about gives you something to talk about as far as what your services, new products, what information they need, where they are having problems, what customer services issues are they are running into with your competitors.

See Addendum – Figure Web 1.13

Brent Leary: Yes

David Bullock: Just by dipping into the conversation gives you a very significant competitive advantage because it gives you marketplace intelligence and this is real time marketplace intelligence. This is not you going to your customers and saying, "Hey, so what's happening in the marketplace." Or "Hey, what are you really concerned about." You are getting people at 2 o'clock in the morning saying, "Oh my gosh, my computer just died I don't know what to do and it's this brand."   Well, you have major companies right now monitoring Twitter to find out where their customer service issues are.

Brent Leary: There's an example of companies actually monitoring Twitter is JetBlue.

David Bullock: Mmhmm

Brent Leary: JetBlue was keeping track of the interest that was on Twitter in respect to the South by Southwest conference, the kind of geeky conference that happens down in Texas. What they were seeing was that not only the interest in the event, but some frustration with not being able to get flights to the event. JetBlue decided to create some flights, some routes for this conference that and they put it out on Twitter and the Twitter community went wild. Thank you so much and JetBlue really got bumped up in the minds of a lot of people because of not only what they did but using Twitter to get a gauge of what was going on in the community and how to positively impact the community.

David Bullock: And it's real time. That part is so interesting. My first experience with Twitter is I was doing a presentation and while I was doing the presentation, the room was tweeting from one side of the room to the other about the presentation as I was doing it. I said "Oh, my gosh."

Brent Leary: Yeah.

David Bullock: Again, this is real time conversation with the marketplace and with so many millions of people on this service, someone out there is talking about, concerned about and engaged with whatever business, whatever concern, whatever event, whatever it is. The key now is to get the information and then figure out how you can engage those people and how can you execute it in a way to consistently get the word out. Twitter allows you to get the word out very easily. 140 characters, boom and it's out there. You'll send them a link, that's your page and you move on.

Brent Leary: Yeah.

David Bullock: I have closed deals and made orders. 140 characters doesn't take that much.

Brent Leary: One thing I will point out is Twitter can drive serious traffic to your website. When I was doing research for an article, I actually had a gentleman on my radio show, Jason Calacanis, who has a company called *Mahalo*. He is one of the leading Twitterers out there and what he said was that he was able to drive twenty thousand people to his website from Twitter.

Read what Jason Calacanis had to say here - http://www.calacanis.com/2008/04/16/twitter-sending-over-20-000-people-a-month-to-mahalo-com/

Now he is a power Twitterer, he's on the upper end and he has thousands of people following him. The possibility is there for you to drive traffic to your business if you use this tool in a strategic manner and that can really impact your bottom line.

 See Addendum – Figure Web 1.14

Your Google Quotient

Does your Web identity represent you as you want to be known?

Build your Google quotient in a way that represents your professional self.

Make an Assessment

- Google your name in quotes to establish a baseline – or basis for comparison

- What's your volume of accurate results?

- How consistently do those results communicate your personal brand?

Based on your evaluation of the below criteria, determine which of the following profiles best describes your current online identity:

Beginner - Absolutely Nothing

Random - Little Information - Negative and Inconsistent

Adversity - Someone Else Shares Your Name. High Volume with Little Relevance

Narrow - Low Volume - High Relevance

Dominant - Reinforces Brand - High Volume

David Bullock: This slide that we're showing you here is really an example of a couple of things. It's showing you that the number of visitors to Barack Obama's website vs. Hillary, as well as the rest of the field that he was working with and you have to say that he's that. It's probably doubled because this is a little bit dated, but at this point when we took this - January moving into May, a three month rolling average, it's almost doubled.

Your Google Quotient

Now the question you have to ask is, what was he doing that the other ones were not doing? He was using the social media. Now look a little bit deeper at the particular graph. I know gender, I know age and I know household income, which means I have full demographic information on the people who are coming to my website. This information is available for you online - not only for your site but also for your competitor's site and more importantly, for your entire market, which means that you can get a gauge of who in the world is your visitor. You will know how to engage them. This is www.compete.com, so it's free, competitive intelligence data that you can go to just by going to www.compete.com. It's great information.   This is great.

 Visit Compete here - http://www.compete.com

We have covered a lot. We try to keep it at a high level because we know that you can only cover so much in forty-five to fifty minutes. We did want to leave you with a couple of things and Barack is a great example, but here are some things that you can do right away to start building what I call your GQ or Google quotient. You are found when people do those searches. We know blogging so we are not even going to cover blogging that is just a great way to get started. It's just in commenting on other peoples' blogs. You want to build your credibility and so if you can identify the leading bloggers in your industry, start reading what they are writing about and seeing what the comments are and add to that conversation that's already taking place. You want to be able to have a conversation on your turf. Before you get a mass of people to your turf, you've got to go to where they are and you have to participate in the ongoing discussions and show that you are a valuable member of that community before you can really make a lot of headway with your own web presence.

Easy Things to Build Up Your GQ
(Google Quotient)

- Comment on popular industry blogs
- Write reviews on www.Amazon.com, www.Epinions.com, etc.
- Participate in conversation already taking place
- Load content on sites like www.ScribD.com and www.Slideshare.net

Brent Leary: I've had a lot of success with writing reviews on Amazon or writing book reviews on my blog. It's really something where www.Epinions.com or www.Hotels.com, anywhere where people are looking for information, you can provide them with it, it starts to build your credibility and gets them interested to potentially engage you on your terms and on your turf.

Also, there are a lot of great sites that will allow you to take information content that you may already have created, like PowerPoint presentations or PDF files or a word documents to begin to upload those files and use those to drive traffic back to you. ScribD.com is a great website which you can upload any kind of file and you can have it go back to you when people see it. They can read it and then click on your website or your blog and it draws traffic back to you. Slideshare.net is another great example. It's the YouTube for PowerPoint presentations.

You can go there and you can upload some of the PowerPoint slides that you feel comfortable about uploading. When you start sharing your content across the web and people start typing your name into Google or whatever search engine you use, your documents are loaded in. It's like SlideShare, and ScribD, and your Facebook page, and your LinkedIn info. All of these things start to show up. When people put your name into Google and nothing comes back... well, David, I'll let you speak on that for yourself, but that's where it ends for me.

David Bullock: Exactly, right now if you're not found on Google, your business name, your name, depends on how you are branding yourself, people Google you. They will Google you. Now, if you type in David Bullock, I show up in the number one spot on Google. I hold the number one and number two position and I have a bunch of positions within the top twenty and it's not only just me and my sites, but it's also people talking about me. A presentation here, a document there and podcast here, that's what you want.

Customer Loyalty

What I set out to do when I came online was start a conversation. You have to go out there. You have to promote. Then after that, if you're engaging enough, the market will start talking about you. When the market starts talking about you, then people will start coming to you and then you can get the expert status that you want in the marketplace.

Brent Leary: You said it is so key - talking about you - but then they will also talk with you.

David Bullock: Exactly

Brent Leary: That's what you want. That is exactly what you want. You need to be able to create time in order to engage people, particularly the right people, in ways that will create value for you. I just popped this up real quick, the pyramids of customer loyalty:

In a nutshell, is you build the best, most valuable relationships with people when you actually have the time to really engage and understand their business. Add value to the point where they view you as more than just a vendor, but they view you as an advocate, a partner, they are a cheerleader for you, and they bring you business. You can only get to that level if you automate as much of the routine processes as you can. Part of the routine in today's world is creating content and distributing content, so you have to find ways that make sense for you that make it easier for you to create the kind of content that will drive people to you and to automate the distribution process of getting that content in the right places.   We talked about a couple of these things, Twitter.   How easy is it to write a sentence and send a button and it goes out to thousands of people?

David Bullock: YouTube, you just upload it and push the button. Google Video is also a video platform, and there is blip.tv. There are many of those platforms out there. This is the best time for businesses to take advantage of the technology, which is out there.

Brent Leary: Yes.

David Bullock: Right now, broadband, fast DSL, cable modem, they are standard. A lot of us are working on Wi-Fi wireless. It's available. Fast broadband is here which means you can get more content across the web. You can get full audio full video moving pictures. You can get it with an air card walking in the airport, going into a Starbucks, it's available. I suspect that at some point all of the connectivity will be free. I think it's because the price is being driven down so far now that there are going to be other ways that that stream is going to be monetized.   You have the reach and the presence.

Brent Leary: At the end of last year, I dedicated my last column for Black Enterprise at the end of 2007 to proclaiming 2008 to be the year of the international solopreneur. That was based on exactly what you said, broadband is prevalent and it's cheap, so we have great access and great pipes laid so that we can move all sorts of big streams of content all around at a very inexpensive rate. There is software as a service. All of these nice applications and free websites and tools that are not only free, but they are easy to use. When you combine those two things, if we can use these two things to automate those routine processes and it allows us to use creative thinking and out of the box thinking to attract and engage the kind of people that we need to in order to make a go at business.   David, I couldn't agree with you more, this is the greatest time for small businesses to really look at how we utilize these tools. Experiment with the tools, you don't have to use them forever. You don't have to use them all. You can experiment and see which ones work for you and then you go full bore into those in an attempt to engage the people that you need to get business done.   Here's the one thing that is out there now. You have online, they index video, they index audio, and they index text, if you put it out there. If you take the time to create the content and you get it out there and promote it. Guess what. It's searchable which means it's findable and almost permanent. It's out there.

Brent Leary: Yeah

David Bullock: The key now is when you put something out there try to think of it doing work for you. It's selling, it's speaking for you, it's putting your message out there and only in that particular situation where you are using something, another platform to communicate to your marketplace, can you communicate to your marketplace. That means that you are not making the sales call. The presale is already done, long before you show up and if you can take anything away from this presentation, that's what Senator Obama did. He put it out there and because he put it out there and then promoted it in other places, people searched for it. They found it and they started talking about it and subsequently you can see it just in his visitor numbers, almost double the first and second places. How can you lose with that type of proposition?

All of these tools are easy to use. You can do it yourself. They are available to you to get in and use the web. The key now is to understand that the Web is a tool, a media for you to use. Don't be scared of it.   You can contact Brent or me. Don't be scared. We can put together the customized plan. We can walk you through how to use these tools because as you can see, we were able to promote this particular webinar on our blogs, the email list. We didn't anything crazy; we just used exactly what we used here. I did a tweet on Twitter for it and it went out.

Brent Leary: Yeah, absolutely. We are going to do one more of these talks and we are going to talk a little bit more about blogging with the three A's and that's analysis, automation and audacity because you need all three to really not just blog effectively, but reach the right people. That is part of blogging effectively. If you are interested, let us know, there's our email addresses. You can check out our blogs too.   We would love to hear some feedback from you on whether this was helpful. We want to make sure that you get something out of it, like David said. It's really important, we don't want to just talk in theory and not have anything for you to be able to practice.   We did get a couple questions about whether the slides will be available. The answer to that is yes. If you are interested in the slides just send me or David an email.   Send it to me because that will make it a little easier for us to coordinate and I'll make sure you get them. David, any last thoughts?

David Bullock: All to say the internet is here, Web 2.0 is here.   We are actually moving to a Web 3.0 situation, take advantage of it. This is the best time. Brent and I stand ready, willing and able to help you work through all of the technicalities, as well as putting together a plan for you and your business. Better yet, not only just put it out there, to also monitor to see if it's actually working for you. With that, we look forward to doing this again for you all in the near future. Please give us some feedback and let us know what you need, want or would like us to cover on the next go around.

Brent Leary: Alright, thanks David, this is great. It was good that we were actually able to run into each other after about 19 years.

David Bullock: Isn't that something.

Brent Leary: We look forward to doing another one for you guys in the near future, thanks again.

David Bullock: Thank you.

Podcast Update #1

Twitter, Video and ScribD

Welcome to our first weekly podcast. With these short audio programs, we'll take a quick look at some of the latest ways the Obama campaign is utilizing social tools and strategies to drive their campaign. Today Obama sent out a tweet from Twitter announcing his new energy plan. This one tweet shifted the entire campaign in terms of use of social media application...

See Addendum – Figure Web 1.15 and 1.16

http://My.BarackObama.com/page/s/firsttoknow

Obama used Twitter to share with his followers where they could see a video where he talks about his new policy. He also included a link to the actual document that was uploaded to his ScribD account:

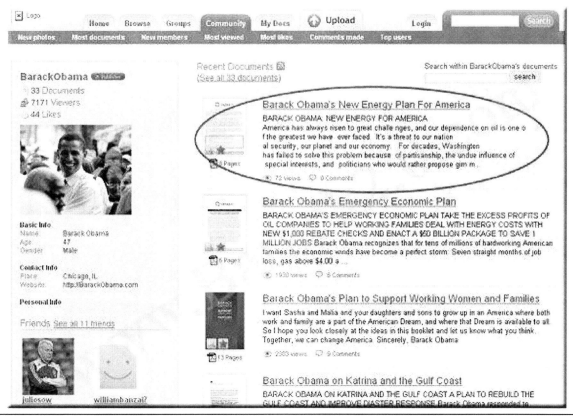

ScribD is a site where you can upload word documents, PDF files, PowerPoint and many other kinds of content that is listed by Google to be included in searches, thus increasing opportunities to drive traffic to your site. One last thing to look at - when we did our first webinar a few weeks back, Obama was being followed by just over 44,000 people on Twitter. Today, according to www.TwitterCounter.com, he has just over 53,000 followers, a 20% increase:

 Visit Barack Obama's Twitter Counter stats here:
http://twittercounter.com/?username=barackobama

Check out this week's podcast as we talk through the lessons you can take from this approach.

 Listen here: http://www.box.net/shared/static/b1n5wj6ogs.mp3

 Barack 2.0 Weekly Update #1
Twitter, Video and ScribD

Brent Leary: Hello, this is Brent Leary and I am here with online business development expert David Bullock. David thanks for joining me man.

David Bullock: Thank you Brent, glad to be here.

Brent Leary: Just last week, we were happy to put out the website www.Barack20.com, which stands for Barack 2.0. It was a couple of weeks ago that we did a webinar on *Barack 2.0 - Social Media Lessons for Business*. Today is our very first Barack 2.0 weekly update. David, tell them what we are going to be doing with this weekly update.

David Bullock: We are actually tracking Barack Obama's campaign and we are extracting the lessons that you can use for your business. Every week, as Senator Obama continues with his campaign, we will be looking at the lessons and actually getting those to you in a way that you can use the properties, the platforms, the strategies and the techniques that he is using to actually move further and further and get attention from the marketplace.

Brent Leary: It just so happens that we were all set to do this first weekly update when we both just so happen to look at Twitter (we both follow Barack Obama from the social media perspective) and we got an update – a tweet – from Barack Obama that says that he is announcing a new energy for America plan.

What's cool about this is that, not only is he using Twitter to announce this plan, but he is also using another service that has the actual document where you can go and read this – it's called www.ScribD.com. If you want to check out this new energy for America plan from Barack Obama's campaign, all you need to do is go to http://www.scribd.com/barackobama.

David, how interesting is that – that he is using, we already talked about him in Twitter in the webinar. We didn't even talk about www.ScribD.com, which is a place where people can upload all sorts of documents that can drive traffic back to their sites.

David Bullock: Let's talk about ScribD for a second, like you said you can upload documents. You are actually feeding the search engines exactly what you want them to see. It's very similar to something called Google Base. Google Base is a situation where you are uploading documents directly into Google's database and saying come look at it. You tag them the way you want them to be tagged. You put the keywords in place. You tell the search engines exactly how you want that document tagged, found and indexed.

More importantly here, you have Barack using three different media in this one Tweet. You have Twitter, which was the announcement mechanism. You have www.my.barackobama.com, which is actually showing the watch it live feed. He has video going here. He is using ScribD to upload a document. He is using Twitter as the announcement mechanism. He is using all three of those synergistically. In one move, you can see how he is using three levels of social media at the same time.

ScribD
Share Your Documents

- Easily publish and share your documents with the world
- Embed documents in any website

ScribD iPaper

- Eliminate bloated document viewers, add-ons, and unsafe downloads.
- Developers can smoothly integrate iPaper documents into websites and applications with little or no additional coding.

Brent Leary: For those of you who are unfamiliar with www.ScribD.com, it's a free setup, you can go and get your account and then you can begin loading stuff that you have already created. If you have some PDFs or Word documents, some PowerPoint that you think would be of interest to drive people to engage you in your business you can set up your own ScribD account and start loading those documents up.

As David said, start tagging them effectively, so when people do a search your stuff comes up. Then hopefully, they like what they see and they transfer over from your ScribD document to your website, your blog or what have you. The interesting thing here is the Barack Obama folks are not new to ScribD, they already have thirty-three documents and those documents have already generated over 7,000 viewers. I am assuming that 7,100 people have checked out one or another or maybe all of these documents.

David Bullock: The other thing that I would like to point out here is when we did our video cast – webinar a couple weeks ago, Barack Obama was only at about 45,000 followers, now he is at 53,000 followers. Something has become very interesting here, he's actually following 55,000 people and he has 53,000 followers. He has actually flipped the situation where he is actually following more people than are following him. Notice, he is using this particular social media platform perfectly.

Brent Leary: David, this has been a great way to start the B20 weekly update. I can't wait until next week. For more information on what's going on with Barack and his social media plan, go to www.Barack20.com. You can download the transcript for the webinar, view the webinar, get the audio of the webinar and you can get the weekly updates.

David Bullock: Oh, and by the way, it is all free. We are not even asking for an email address or anything. This is information to help you to build your businesses. We hope to see you there. Please, if you have any comments, please feel free to leave comments on the blog; we would love to hear from you.

Brent Leary: Once again, this is the Barack 2.0 weekly update.

Podcast Update #2

Using Text Messaging to Announce VP Pick

On Sunday, August 10, 2008, the Obama campaign used Twitter to inform followers that their VP pick would be announced sometime between now and the start of the Democratic convention. The way that this is being handled is causing significant buzz in the marketplace...

BarackObama

✓ Following − Device updates OFF

Announcing the VP candidate sometime between now & the Convention by txt msg & email. Text VP to 62262 or visit http://my.barackobama.com/vp

The interesting thing here is the offer the campaign is making. If you want to be among the first to hear whom Obama's tapping to be his vice president, you can sign up to receive a text message or email notification.

Below is the sign up for to receive an email notification:
http://My.BarackObama.com/page/s/firsttoknow

 See Addendum – Figure Web 1.17

The use of text messaging to instantly communicate information of value to those you wish to engage creates opportunities to learn more about them. In addition, by giving people the option of whether to email or text them, you learn which method of communication they prefer. Just as the Obama campaign offered people interested in being the "first to know" opportunity when they provided contact information, you can do that as well.

A good business example of this is what Borders has done. You can sign up for their free Borders Rewards Club by providing some basic contact information. By doing this, they send out emails with discount coupons of up to 40% off. That was nice but it was still inconvenient having to print the coupon off and bring it into the store. Sometimes I'd be in the store when I would receive the email and had no way to use it. Borders started offering text message coupons, and all you have to do is show the text message to the cashier and they would immediately apply the discount. I went with the text message offer, while I'm sure those who prefer email stuck with that. You may want to think of ways you can entice customers and prospects to let you communicate with them via text messages and/or email. It's cost effective and keeps you instantly connected. More and more people will initially read their messages on mobile devices. But it's important to let them make the call on how they want to be reached, which is why the Obama campaign was smart to let people sign up for either text or email option.

Also capturing contact information is as easy as creating a basic web page that is integrated into a service like Zoho CRM or Microsoft Office Live Small Business.

    Visit Zoho CRM at: http://crm.zoho.com/

For example Zoho, free for the first three users in a company, has a function that allows you to generate a contact form that pushes the information submitted on your web page directly into your Zoho CRM account. You'll have a central location for the contact information you'll collect, which is critically important. You can also set up auto-responders to let people know you received their information. One last thing, don't let typing stop you from sending text messages and using sites like Twitter.

    Visit Jott at: http://www.jott.com/

You can use a free service like Jott, which will actually let you create and send text messages by creating a voice message. Your voice message will be translated into a text message and will be sent out on your behalf.

Check out this week's podcast as we talk through the lessons you can take from this approach.

    Listen here: http://www.box.net/shared/static/tq5zxnzcqu.mp3

    Barack 2.0 Weekly Update #2
Using Text Messaging to Announce VP Pick

Brent Leary: Welcome to the second installment of the Barack 2.0 weekly update. I'm Brent Leary and I have with me my buddy David Bullock. David, how are you doing man?

David Bullock: I am fine and glad to be here again to give you an update.

Brent Leary: Last week we talked a little bit about how he is using Twitter. Well, they are announcing the VP candidate sometime between now and convention. I think that the convention is the later part of this month. He put that out on Twitter, but the curious thing is, if you want to know the instant they announce whoever the VP is, you can sign up and get it via text message.

David, talk a little bit about how that is interesting and how that is something that small business could actually do around this as well.

David Bullock: That gets into what they call mobile messaging. Everyone has a cell phone now and as you know, on those cell phones, you can get a text message. He is bridging the gap between what is happening online to what is actually happening in your hand offline. It doesn't matter where you are. You could be in a restaurant, the job, you could be anywhere and you can still get that information. You are getting that information pushed to you because you requested it to where? Your personal cell phone. As you know, just about everyone has a cell phone and some people even have two. You see that we have gone with this text messaging as a discreet way to pass information from one to another. Barack's campaign has now moved from offline to online and is actually bridging that gap.

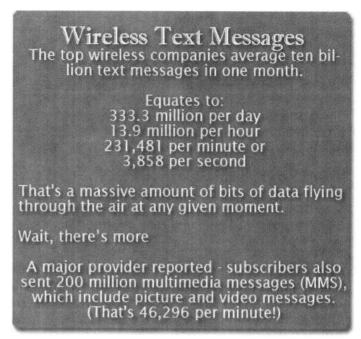

Now, as far as you being a small business, one of the things that you can do is get the cell phone numbers of your clients, of your customers and if you have something that you would like them to know about, a special, a sale, you need to get to them. What is the best way to get to someone? Via their cell phone.

Brent Leary: An example that I love to use – I love Borders, and I know this is a big company but this is an example that anybody can use. They have the Borders Reward Club. You just sign up and give your contact information, your email address and all that kind of thing. They had been sending out these special discounts – 25% off here 35% off there on books or DVDs or whatever and you had been getting them via email. I like getting those emails, but I didn't like the fact that I had to print the stuff off, where if I just so happen to be in Borders and I got the email, I don't have a way to print off the thing, so I can't use it while I am there.

What Borders did, which I think is a stroke of genius, is started asking if you would rather start receiving text message discounts. Instead of having to print off the discount coupon all you have to do now is pick up the item, show them your text message on your mobile device and they write down the code and you instantly get your 25-40% off, whatever it is.

David Bullock: Wow, look at something else there, there is a cost savings. They push out something electronically and you don't have to print anything up, there's no flyer, there's no special card to punch. It goes right from the computer to the cell phone. There are a couple of tools that are out there that we talked about like www.Jott.com. A friend of mine can actually speak a message to me on his cell phone and it is emailed to me directly and/or sent straight to a text message. At this point, the technology does exist for us to be able to instantly connect with the information that we want and better yet, as a business owner you can connect with your clients and customers with special offers, very discreetly at little to no cost.

Brent Leary: Borders is a big company, but hey, dry cleaners can do the same thing. A pizza shop owner could too. If you collect any type of contact information, if you have a special on a pizza, send it out via text message and say hey, bring this text message in, get 25% off.

David Bullock: There's a piece there that's an underlying part, before you can send the messages out, you have got to collect the names, phone numbers and email addresses. Many times business owners aren't collecting that information. If you don't collect it, you don't have any way to send stuff out. Build that list to a couple hundred or a couple thousand. Those are all people who said; "Yes, I want to hear from you." "Yes, send me information." They are ready, willing and able. I know we are talking about what to do with it, but before you can do something with it, you have to collect the information first.

Brent Leary: People love discounts, you have to give them an incentive to give up their contact information, believe me if someone is going to give me 35% off of something I really want, I am more then happy to give you my text message number, phone number, anything. Think of ways to entice people to give you that information.

Once again, David hit it right on the head, your communication costs go down, because you don't have to worry about getting things printed up. All you have to do is transmit the message and it goes out to any number of people. Your costs have been lowered and you have also increased the satisfaction from the customer's perspective. I love it. I love the fact that I don't have to go and print something now, all I have to do is show them my phone and I get 40% off.

David Bullock: You are walking around with a discount card that has any number of discounts on it right there. The question is, you as a business owner, are you going to be one of the people offering one of those discounts to one of your clients?

Brent Leary: That is the message today, Barack used Twitter and text messaging to put out information, but he also invited people to say hey, if you want to be the first to know about something, sign up and we'll make sure that we get you that information as soon as it comes out. As business people, we can look at that and say, we can do the same kind of thing. We want to engage our customers and build our customer relationships. We should be using all the things that customers expect. That might be working with a cell phone or a mobile device, shooting information out, letting them receive in the fashion that they want to get it in, and letting them use it to get the kind of product and service they want from us.

 Find out who is the most popular on Twitter, or check your own stats here: http://www.twitterholic.com/

David Bullock: Just very quick as far as an update on Twitter, we are looking here at a tool called www.TwitterHolic.com, which ranks where people are as far as followers and friends and updates on Twitter. Right now, the Barack Obama campaign is at 55,509 followers. He is in the number two position. The person right above him is at 56,072. We suspect within the next week, week and a half, the Obama campaign or the Obama account on Twitter will be on the number one spot on the Twitter platform.

"Great website. It has been fun to watch Barack use text messaging. As the text advisors for the Hillary Clinton campaign, we can only wish that the campaign would have done all that we outlined to them, which Barack did in his campaign. Sen. Clinton did however get the religion toward the end of the campaign and began using the service much more effectively."

Michael Anderson - www.interlinkedmedia.com

Podcast Update #3

MiGente.com: Barack and his 54,000 Other Online Friends

On last week's update, we pointed out that Barack was about 500 followers short of becoming the most followed person on Twitter. It didn't take long for him to jump into the number one spot, as many media outlets pointed out - even www.TechCrunch.com covered it the day he took the top spot. Obama now has more than 59,000 followers - over 2,000 more followers than the number two person on the list, Digg's Kevin Rose.

While much has been made of Obama's following on Twitter, Facebook and other "mainstream" social networking sites, there are other lesser-known sites that he is participating in just as actively. MiGente.com is a great example of a social site Obama is a member of that doesn't have the hype of the larger social networking sites.

  Visit MiGente here: http://www.migente.com/

  See Addendum – Figure Web 1.18

MiGente.com is a social site dedicated to serving the Latino community. It's a great looking site with all the functionality of the bigger-name sites. What it has that the other sites lack is the singular focus on the Latino community, the issues of importance to them, and content that appeals to their community. With the Latino vote being critical in the upcoming election, it makes a great deal of sense to reach out to them - where they are, in ways that are comfortable to them.

  See Addendum – Figure Web 1.19

While TechCrunch heralded Obama's rise to the top of Twitter with over 59,000 followers, they didn't report that he has almost as many friends (almost **54,000**) on www.MiGente.com. To us, this is equally as noteworthy as the Twitter news and maybe even more interesting from a small business perspective because small business people need to participate in social networks that fit the niches our customers and prospects participate in. In many cases, these more focused sites can provide deeper, more meaningful interactions that could accelerate relationship building. Therefore, while you work Twitter, Facebook, LinkedIn and other major social networks, don't ignore the www.MiGente.com's of the world that represent niches in your field/industry. Barack didn't.

Check out this week's podcast as we talk through the lessons you can take from this approach.

 Listen here: http://www.box.net/shared/static/qehc8xcglu.mp3

 Barack 2.0 Weekly Update #3
MiGente.com: Barack and his 54,000 Other Online Friends

Brent Leary: Welcome to the third edition of the Barack 2.0 Weekly Update. I am Brent Leary and with me, as always, is David Bullock. David, how are you today?

David Bullock: I am well, glad to be here again.

Brent Leary: Last week when we did this, I believe Barack was about five or six hundred followers behind Kevin Rose, according to www.TwitterHolic.com, so why don't we just go ahead and take care of that up front. What is the update for this week?

David Bullock: The update now is Barack Obama has 59,473 followers. Kevin Rose has 57,341 followers. As of right now, Barack Obama is the most followed person on the planet on Twitter by well over 2,000 followers and obviously, that number is going to grow continually.

Brent Leary: That might not seem like a big deal, but it really is.   Kevin Rose is one of the A list personalities in social media because he is one of the co-founders of www.Digg.com. I would say that maybe six months ago, there was no way Barack was anywhere near where this guy is or near the top period.

David Bullock: Exactly, we are looking at a situation where if you look at followers and you again frame this in terms of a business application, those followers really turn out to be your mailing list. Those people have raised their hands and said that I want to hear from you. Anything that you say, I'd like to at least be in the position to get that information from you. What that means is that Barack Obama has people that have volunteered and said we want to hear from you. That is 59,000 people.   Here is where it gets interesting. The viral effect of opinion is such that if he has that many core people talking about him and wanting to hear from him that influences two or three levels deep in the marketplace.

Brent Leary: In addition to being great when it comes to using the big guys like Facebook, Twitter and all the other big time social networks, he has also targeted out specific niche social networks so that he can connect with people on a different level that you might not be able to do on the more general social network. One of those that I just sort of came across and I give all the credit to my niece who was down visiting last week and she is getting her Masters in some sort of Spanish curriculum, she is heavily into the Latino culture. She was on the web and she pointed me to a site called MiGente. I decided that I was going to see what this was about and lo and behold on the home page, they have a section they call the featured members section. David would you care to take a guess as to who the featured member was when I went to that page?

David Bullock: I will gander that it was Senator Obama.

Brent Leary: It really surprised me. I was not expecting to see that.   What it shows is that he and his campaign understand the value of connecting with people on their turf. It's critically important, if you are trying to do business with people or trying to building relationships with people, find out where they are, where they spend their time, not just feet in the street but actually online, where they spend their time. If they are a member of a specific social network, there may be a more niched social network that they really feel engaged and feel like they are a member of the community and they need to find for themselves or their business. I think that is a great lesson for all small businesses. Don't stop at the general mainstream that everyone knows about. Do your homework; find out from the people that you would like to do business with where they are hanging out on the web. Then build your presence there, because you want to meet them where they feel most comfortable.

David Bullock: That lesson is so powerful in that Senator Obama is showing up where the people are – repeatedly. The idea of him being ubiquitous is becoming more prevalent because he is up high and you look in the niches and he is there too. These people can also say he is here for me.   Again, he is developing relationships, almost a one on one relationship with thousands of people across multiple media because that is possible now using the social media applications and platforms that are available.

Brent Leary: The other point that is very interesting, we just talked about how he is leading the pack on Twitter with almost 60,000 followers. How many people have friended him on MiGente, this is really interesting to me, almost as many people have friended him on MiGente as he has following on Twitter. He has got close to 54,000 people on MiGente that have friended him. We don't talk about politics here, but one of the things that I remember coming up through the primaries, how it seemed like he had an issue connecting with the Latinos. Well, 54,000 on one social networking site have befriended him in that community. That tells me that he is at the very least reaching out, trying to connect with them in ways that seem to be working.

David Bullock: That effort that we see in the trying to. It's not hard at all to connect now, because you can do it online. It's not that you have to get in the car and kiss any babies, you don't have to do all that campaigning. But he is doing that too, in addition to all of the social networking that is going on. Some people may never, ever meet him in person but they will feel as though they have a relationship with him because of meeting him through the social media.

Brent Leary: Absolutely, one last point on the whole MiGente thing, actually it's a really nice social networking site.

David Bullock: It is nice.

Brent Leary: I would say go check it out when you get a chance, but one of the cool things and this is another of these lessons is that on his profile, he has loaded up a lot of his content. Although he has created content that may seem to be suited for CNN or what have you. He is also able to place that content that was already created and put it over in this community, so they can see it on their mechanism of communication and collaboration. It's about creating good content and also placing it where the people you want to associate with will consume it and collaborate with you and hold a conversation with you. That's great, creating good content, but also placing it where it can be consumed is incredibly important.

Content Repurposing

Here are just a handful of different formats and uses for repurposing of your content:

Articles
Audios
Blogs
Books
eBooks
eCourses
Home Study Courses
Membership Sites

Podcasts
Press Releases
Special Reports
Teleseminars
Tips Booklets
Transcripts
Videos

David Bullock: There's an additional piece that you bring up here called repurposing. Just because you have your content in one place, for instance here; we have the audio, video, transcript. It is the same content morphed into different forms so that the people that are tactile can read it. Those auditory listeners can hear it. The people that are visual can see it - notice, same content – purposed across the media for ease of consumption. That is the part, which is phenomenal to me because you can actually take something that you have and have it work for you extremely hard because you are getting to your clients in a way that they can actually consume it. Brent, you make a great point and that's called repurposing. Every business owner should be looking at how they might use this repeatedly because it's evergreen material. You should want to use it repeatedly. You will get tired of your marketing materials and you will get tired of your sales materials long before your market will ever get tired of your sales and marketing materials.

Brent Leary: Absolutely. The last thing we talked about in the weekly update from last week. How he had reached out via Twitter to tell folks that they are going to announce their VP at some point between now and the convention and if you wanted to be the first ones to get the word, you can sign up for either a text message or email. We didn't get a chance to talk about the word of mouth and buzz because it had just come out. David, tell them a little bit about the word-of-mouth and buzz that came out of the one Tweet.

David Bullock: It showed up on every media on the planet, from the Wall Street Journal down to CNN, talking about how he is going to do this. Then there were studies that were being done with communication professors at the university level, saying look at how he is communicating with the marketplace. Let's look at it a little bit deeper. People are waiting anxiously, so they place a value on the information. Now the media itself has become the message. When is it is coming? That anticipation, that creating of value, has created yet another underlying piece of news that is permeating in the marketplace. From a business owner's standpoint, "what can you do to create an almost movie-like buzz before the movie is even released for your product?" That is exactly what Senator Obama is doing at this point in his campaign, creating anticipation. They want it before they can even have it.

Brent Leary: That is a business lesson folks, everything that David just talked about applies to us as small business people. We can use all of these mechanisms, but we have to do it strategically, so we are hitting the goal. The goal is to make ourselves available and engage people who we think would make for great business partners for customers and us and that is exactly the lessons that I am seeing and David, I think you are seeing it as well in all these little moves we talk about when it comes to this weekly update.

This has been great. We have only been doing this for three weeks. Take a look at all the lessons that the folks that have listened to us are learning and we are learning as well.

David Bullock: That's the part, as you can see, as we are seeing this unfold on a global stage. This case study is happening right now. We are seeing all these nuances of anticipation and repurposing. How do you show up in front of your customer? Where do you show up? Do you meet them at home or do you make them come to you? What is push marketing? What is pull marketing? A complete MBA course is being played out right before our eyes.

Brent Leary: Luckily, we are just along for the ride, we are checking it out and we hope that you are enjoying these weekly updates. We have come to the end of this one, but rest assured there will be another one next week. David, any last parting words before we head out for another week?

David Bullock: Again, keep your eyes open, we will be doing more and more of this and these calls become more and more in depth as we move closer and closer to the actual date of the election, because I suspect there will be more deep seated ramifications and lessons that you can use immediately. Again, we hope that you are hearing these and going back and looking at your market and what is happening in the marketplace and actually starting to do stuff now because that is the purpose. We look forward to talking to you very soon.

Brent Leary: Comment – we want some comments folks.

David Bullock: Oh yes, please come to the blog. We have gotten well over two hundred – three hundred downloads of the transcript and other materials. We want to hear from you. How are you using this information to increase your reach in the marketplace? You all have great ideas, we know you are doing things; we are just reporting to the marketplace and hopefully giving you the spark where you can become active within your business.

Brent Leary: This has been another Barack 2.0 weekly update. See you next week.

Brent Leary and David Bullock

Podcast Update #4

Marketing Power of Domain Names

We do our weekly check on how many folks are following Senator Obama on Twitter, and touch on the impact of the text message announcing the choice of Joe Biden as Obama's running mate.

Obama's Text Message

From: 622-62

Barack has chosen Senator Joe Biden to be our VP nominee. Watch the first Obama-Biden rally live at 3pm ET on www.BarackObama.com. Spread the word!

August 23, 3:29 AM

August 23, 2008

We look at the impact the text message announcement had on Sprint

http://www.betanews.com/article/Could_Obamas_VP_pick_have_triggered_millions_in_SMS_traffic/1219772300

See Addendum – Figure Web 1.20

We discuss a very interesting Washington Post article discussing in detail the role social media played in the Obama campaign. We also look at www.FightTheSmears.com and discuss the importance of picking the right domain names from a small business marketing perspective.

Read the Washington Post Article here: http://www.washingtonpost.com/wp-dyn/content/article/2008/08/19/AR2008081903186.html

See Addendum – Figure Web 1.21

You may also want to check out this related article:

http://www.smallbiztrends.com/2007/12/master-of-my-domain-names.html/

Check out this week's podcast as we talk through the lessons you can take from this approach.

Listen here: http://www.box.net/shared/static/f9s64k4d1k.mp3

Barack 2.0 Weekly Update #4
Marketing Power of Domain Names

Brent Leary: Welcome to the fourth installment of the Barack 2.0 Weekly Update. I'm Brent Leary and as always, business development expert extraordinaire guru David Bullock. How are you doing man?

David Bullock: Brent, I am well. Glad to be here we have a lot to talk about today Sir.

Brent Leary: Yeah, but before we get into it, it was good seeing you over the weekend, coming to Atlanta, Georgia.

David Bullock: Yeah, it's a wonderful city. It's good to sit around with people who actually know what social media and internet marketing is all about and how it all works.

Brent Leary: What was cool is we were able to meet a guy that we actually talked about and featured in our Barack 2.0 webinar, which is SEO rapper Chuck Lewis. That was really cool meeting him.

David Bullock: Yeah, it was good to meet him, but as some of our listeners know he started by putting a YouTube video up. It really came to a head this weekend in that he was offered a position with an internet marketing organization, because he got the attention of the marketplace from those videos that he did.

Brent Leary: Absolutely, once again, that is a single small business guy, using video in a unique way, that captivated people and it brought him contracts and jobs. That's a great thing. Let's get into it a little bit. We always do this weekly update of how Barack is being tracked and followed on Twitter. What is the number this week?

David Bullock: It's well over 65,000.

Brent Leary: Wow

David Bullock: He just surpassed the biggest players in the marketplace that had a little bit over 50,000. He jumped passed them with about 10,000 followers on Twitter.

Brent Leary: Now, when we first started talking, he was in third or fourth place, significantly behind. Now he is over 6,000 ahead of the next guy.

David Bullock: The closest follower is Kevin Rose who has 59,319 and Barack Obama is at 65,101 people. He soared past the people, the founders of many of the large social media spaces that people refer to on a day-to-day basis.

Brent Leary: That is very important because of what we are going to talk about next. The whole VP announcement and the text message that actually began with a tweet from Twitter. It happened over the weekend. It went out to I don't know how many people but there were so many people that something happened at Sprint... do you know what really happened there?

David Bullock: Sprint has such a surge in text messaging that they had a little interruption in their system. Not so much that the system went down, but the messages did not come over instantaneously. Some of the messages actually were delayed and they could not get them out fast enough, but that just says that one move overtaxed the system that had been in place. What happened had never been done before, not that way.

Brent Leary: The fact that he was able to use Twitter to say to folks, if you want to be one of the first to know who our VP choice is, sign up for a text message or an email. Twitter is free, so he put that message out free and he got all kinds of people signing up for it free. Then he sent out the text message – I don't know how text messages work, but if you sent it out – even if it is going to a 100 thousand people, do you just get charged once for the one send out?

David Bullock: That's a special service, but I believe that you get charged for every message that goes out.

Brent Leary: Oh, okay.

David Bullock: Now, I don't know what that charge would be, there is bulk buying and there is always a supply and demand issue. Again, the fact is that this is a very cheap and inexpensive way to get a message out. It's point-to-point communication and all the message said was that Senator Barack Obama has selected Joe Biden as our VP candidate – watch the first rally live at 3pm – go to this website. Here is the vital part, the text message then said spread the word. You have the information and a call to action exactly where to go and what to do with the message.

Brent Leary: The good thing about it too is, although you could have gotten the text message, you could have also had signed up for the email. We all know how cheap email is.

David Bullock: Free

Brent Leary: Either way it is either low cost or no cost and the other cool thing about it is, now that he has their information, chances are he is probably going to send them more than just that last text message.

David Bullock: He has grabbed that information, which means they are now in the database, which means ongoing communication is a possibility for a very long time.

Brent Leary: That's a great lesson for us small business people - how we can put something out on Twitter and have people put a nice little URL or a little tease, if you want some more information – use this link and have a nice landing page set up for when people click on it. Make it enticing enough so that once they get there, they do what you want them to do and that's to provide the contact information to you and then you can begin communicating with them on a regular basis. That is business, that's not politics, that's business.

David Bullock: That's building a list of the people that want to hear from you so that you can make offers.

Brent Leary: That's a beautiful thing. It's a beautiful example of how we can use things that are low cost or no cost to communicate effectively with people we want to do business with. That's great.

David Bullock: Mmhmm

Brent Leary: Something that caught our attention last week, from the Washington Post of all places, an extensive online article that really outlined the strategy of how the Obama team looked at social media and how they used it to get to where they are right now. What was your take away from that article?

David Bullock: A couple of things, the article actually came out on Wednesday, August 20, 2008. Two take-aways, Obama has a team behind him that really understands the space. The nice thing is this very story echoes what Brent and I have been bringing to you all for the last several weeks. The social media space is here and if you know how to utilize it well, you will get the attention of not only the small marketplace, but also the big marketplace. We will put the link to that article on our website so that you can see it.

Read the Washington Post Article here: http://www.washingtonpost.com/wp dyn/content/article/2008/08/19/AR2008081903186.html

The exciting part for me Brent was that what we were seeing is what the Washington Post was reporting on, except they weren't framing it on how you could use it as a business owner. They were looking strictly from a political promotional standpoint. Again, we want you to frame this information. So what can you do with your business?

Brent Leary: It's a must read for folks, but you need to read it in the context of what it can do for you.

David Bullock: Most definitely, because if you read that article and you look at how we have outlined the website, you can follow this blueprint.

Brent Leary: It's good stuff. We will have a link to that article as a part of this weekly podcast and blog. One of the things that we really wanted to talk about today and spend a few minutes on is the whole idea of buying domains and what Barack has done around that is really interesting. Of course, he has the www.BarackObama.com domain, but he also did something at the beginning of June when it started focusing on the general election and politics is politics and people started putting stuff out there. The Obama campaign side put together a site called FightTheSmears.com. David, that's a really interesting domain itself, but having the domain and find the right words and putting a website up, there is a great story for small businesses behind that.

David Bullock: Absolutely, when you are looking at your domain name, you have to ask the question of what do you want this web property to actually do. In this particular case, that domain name was bought on June 1, 2008. That domain was bought quickly and immediately to fill a need in the particular campaign that Senator Obama was in. He wanted to have a presence online that people could use and refer to fight what he knew was going to be coming as he moved further into the promotional piece of the Presidency.

Strategically he bought the name, fight the smears. There is a website there. It is viral in nature. It has good information to counter any of the other information in the marketplace, he can use that to promote himself and his campaign against what is happening in the marketplace. If you are a business owner and all of the sudden you started seeing negative PR, you have to do reputation management. It is very easy for you to go and pick up a domain name and start putting your information there and start referring people away from you to a seemingly third party that validates your position in the marketplace.

Brent Leary: It's really key and critical for small business people to understand how important in the marketing of your small business a domain name can be. Because we all know at this point, when people are looking for product or service information, the first place they are going to is to the web. They are going to their search engine of choice, be it Google, Ask, MSN , Yahoo whatever it is and they are putting in words, because those words – they are hoping will lead to help in whatever they are trying to do.

If you think about it in those terms, you need to get a great domain that makes sense that will connect with the people that are searching for the products and services that you deliver. It can be anything like fight the smears. That doesn't say Barack Obama fights the smears. It just says fight the smears and in that context, that is what it is.

Choosing A Domain Name

- Register www.yourname.com

A good domain name should be:

- Easy to remember
- Easy to spell

The name of your company is always a good choice. If your desired domain name is already taken, you can search if the .net or .org variation is available. You may also use hyphens to create unique domain names.

For example, both David and I have our names, so you can go to www.DavidBullock.com and you'll see a site. You can go to www.BrentLeary.com and you'll see a site. One of the things that you might want to do right off the bat as a small businessperson is get your name.

David Bullock: Get your name and get your company name, because as we are moving now, people buy from people and they want to connect within the visual, so maybe having your name may be the best PR that you have. It's always interesting when you pass someone your card and it's your name dot com. That says a lot about how you are positioned in the marketplace.

Brent Leary: I would say that it even goes a little bit further because, as a small businessperson, when people are looking to your small business, like David said, they are looking to you. They are looking to the individual. You represent this small business. Even if you have five or ten employees, it's representing you and when they do a search on your name, something better come up. If your name doesn't come up, that's just not good. I know that when I go to networking event and I get a card from somebody that I have been talking to, I look their name up first. I don't look for their business, I do that second. I look up their name up first and I bet the majority of people do that as well.

David Bullock: People go to Google as the authority to who, what, when, why and how. They are the information repository of probably the world right now. They have the data, at least in the United States and I think you called it the Google quotient - The GQ. Who are you in the eyes of Google and if you're not taking the time to put stuff out there about you, then the rest of the world will. You want to make sure that it's good stuff.

Brent Leary: Absolutely, and you want to show up. It just doesn't look good to put a name in – I'm telling you, if I put a name in and nothing comes back, I don't have enough time in the day to mess around. There are too many good people out there that when I put their name in and good stuff comes back that I want to build relationships with.

David Bullock: Understood.

Brent Leary: The other piece of that is – if you are trying to come up with a marketing campaign for your product or service, find a domain name that may drive traffic to it. I think that's very critical. People take a lot of time finding the right name for their domains. I know I do. I probably buy three or four domains a month. I don't know when I am going to use it, but if I can find something and spend seven dollars that could turn into something really big. I can afford to play hit or miss.

David Bullock: Having a domain name is owning property. There is a whole business around domaining for people that just buy vanity domain names that have type in traffic. People just type in tennis shoes or sneakers and that should bring up exactly what they want. There is a whole slew of thought behind picking the right domain name. The long and short of it is don't be afraid to spend the nine dollars or ten dollars to go get a domain name, because that domain name could be valuable, not just from you selling the domain to someone else, but building your property there. The other thing, I just spoke at a seminar this weekend, websites – plural. If you are going to dominate your niches, you need web properties in the keyword set to go dominate a market. You cannot do that if you are only dealing with one property and only concentrating there.

Brent Leary: Great advice. That's all I can say, great advice. Cheap and easy is good folks – it can drive a lot of traffic to your sites. So definitely get the domain. Spend some time figuring out what will be a great domain that will act as a piece of marketing collateral for your business. We have come to another end of a Barack 2.0 Weekly Update. We are packing a lot of stuff in here, but there is so much to pack.

David Bullock: Many things are going on in the marketplace. The technology is changing and Senator Obama is using the social networking side or Web 2.0 side very well. We are just trying to document this so you know what we see when we are moving in the marketplace and what you can use for your business.

Brent Leary: Well, until next week, that will be the first one after this convention, I am sure we will have a lot to talk about that will come out of that from a social media perspective.

David Bullock: Exactly, we will have a lot after the convention.

Brent Leary: As always, folks we want to hear from you, leave some comments. You have been listening to the latest Barack 2.0 Weekly Update. See you next week.

Podcast Update #5

Lessons From the
Democratic National Convention

This week we're glad to have a conversation with James Andrews. James is Vice President at Ketchum Interactive, specializing in the creation of online media/blogger strategy, web/application development, and content production. James is also Founder of www.TheKeyinfluencer.com. Additionally, James is an Expert Blogger for www.FastCompany.com.

With his unique perspective as a social media expert, James shares with us his professional and personal experiences attending last week's Democratic National Convention. James fills us in on how social media infused the event, how the Democrats embraced the blogging community, and how he used Twitter and Facebook to connect with people while at the convention.

He also shares lessons he wants small businesses to learn from the Obama campaign's strategic use of mobile messaging, as well as social media. We also had the honor of having our original Barack 2.0 slide presentation featured on the homepage of SlideShare.net the last week of August 2008.

Check out this week's podcast as we talk through the lessons you can take from this approach.

 Listen here: http://www.box.net/shared/static/nsjdqhcj0o.mp3

 Barack 2.0 Weekly Update #5
Lessons from the DNC

Brent Leary: Hello and welcome to the fifth installment of the Barack 2.0 Weekly Update. I am Brent Leary and unfortunately, today I do not have with me my partner in all this David Bullock the online business expert guru. Fortunately enough for me, I have somebody who can help me out and his name is James Andrews. James is the VP of interactive media for Ketchum and he is the founder of www.TheKeyinfluencer.com. James, thank you for joining me here today man.

James Andrews: Hey, thanks for having me, appreciate it.

Brent Leary: One of the things that I really want to talk to you about is what you did last week. You were at the Democratic national convention and I wanted to get your impressions on what went on and what was it like out there and taking in what was going on.

James Andrews: Well, first of all, it was probably one of the most fulfilling experiences I have ever been a part of in my life. Just as an American, as a human being. I know those are very big words, but one of the first times in my adult life that I ever felt so patriotic. It was an amazing experience. I have to tip my hat to the Democratic Party and to Barack Obama for making all of us feel like one.

For instance, in the Invesco Field last day speech that many people saw, I said to one of my colleagues, I have never been a stadium or environment, especially with African Americans who were actually waving American flags and singing *Born in the USA* and really feeling excited about this country.

I grew up a completely different way and for me the fact that I was there, proud to be an American, proud of what we were going through, it was just an amazing experience. I was excited about and something that I really came back and was able to talk to my kids about. It was something I will never forget, whether Barack is elected or not. So the main thing, I think the support of Barack, The City of Denver was a wonderful host city, very clean, very open to people coming from around the world to celebrate. It was all about Barack.

I can tell you of a bunch of parties, Ben Affleck and Hill Harper did something or another event with Hill Harper and that Biz Markie DJ. On any given night, you had to choose between Bono, Kanye – pick a celebrity. It was an amazing nightlife experience for a political event. I come from an entertainment background so I am used to big parties, but I was shocked to see the number of great parties that happened.

Brent Leary: Wow

James Andrews: Then just the people on fire for causes, tons of protests and things were happening there. I think Colorado was a great state for a liberal platform. There was a bunch of inherent liberal values that live in Colorado. It was a great opportunity to ignite some passionate folks who were on fire for causes. Rage Against the Machine did a concert in the park, the riot gear was out, it was just great. It was a great experience.

Brent Leary: Wow, in addition to the personal experiences that you just related and that was awesome, getting that first hand experience that I wasn't able to make it. It's interesting to get your perspective on it. Now put on your professional hat, because they actually had some things going on where they were asking people to reach out to folks who were there - to reach out and help folks to make them feel a part of this as well.   How did that play into it and how important is this social media aspect of what they are doing with their campaign?

James Andrews: Well, I think again, hats off to what you are doing because it really confirms the importance of Barack's social media strategy, more then just even being a political candidate. I think it's a model that we'll be looking at for years to come on how to build a brand. I think that Barack and the Democratic Party did a great job of extending an arm out to bloggers. They had a blogger's tent set up. I wasn't part of the blogger's tent so I can only speak of it externally. But they had a bloggers tent set up and a bunch of activities for bloggers. They had spaces where people were uploading and shooting YouTube videos and then there were just active movements and a great presence by some great prolific and important bloggers in the space.

The Denver Seven come to mind, a group of African American bloggers that were there blogging about what was happening there. They actually set up a website called the *Denver Seven*. It was just an amazing – a sign of the times. You had traditional media and then you had new media all converging in the same place and all with credentials, because as you know in places like the Democratic National Convention it's very difficult to obtain credentials. The fact that bloggers actually had credentials was an amazing feat, and I think that it says a lot about the Democratic Party and the important that they see that the blogosphere and social media plays.

  To visit the Denver Seven, please visit: http://thedenver7.blogspot.com/

Then you had people like me that were just out there for a number of reasons, but one of which was to work with Hill Harper who was able to launch a website that we helped launch that was called www.ForRealSolutions.com, where we were just doing renegade shooting with our camera and doing some live web streaming stuff. You had a number of people like us that weren't necessarily part of the official credential crew, but were doing some of the content capture.

Brent Leary: What was interesting, from my perspective, sitting here in Atlanta and seeing what was going on, on Twitter – the UStream video, just seeing all of the interactivity and engagement that people were doing when they were out there and giving their take on what was going on.

In addition to having things like CNN and MSNBC and other news networks, what I liked was the one on one engagement, the stories that were coming out from the people that were the feet on the street. That was key to my understanding of what people were feeling from more of an individual perspective.

James Andrews: Yeah, it was amazing. There was Shepard Fairey, who is famous for the Obama campaign (he is a graffiti artist that does a bunch of really great artwork) had an art show called *Manifest Hope Gallery*, really, really beautiful pieces on Obama. You have probably seen his shirt that says, "Hope" underneath. It's interesting because my whole "cool kid crew" from L.A. were at Shep's gallery, and I wouldn't have known about Shep's art show had I not seen their status updates on Facebook.

From an individual base, moving around the city, I was able to be in the right places because people knew I was actually in Denver from my status updates. Ironically, I went to Denver without any credentials and had no problems attending everything because people that are friends with me on Facebook, who work with the DNC and produce events, unbeknownst to me, actually hit me up after I put Denver on my status update and made me come and pick up credentials.

Brent Leary: Now that's awesome.

James Andrews: Yeah, it was really cool. I was actually able to see the speech because one of my friends said "you're in Denver? You need to get down here right now and I have credentials waiting for you." I guess I am so engrained and inherent in what I do on a day-to-day basis, to stop and think about it. For the people who are professionals, like Bara Tunday, who was a great blogger out there doing great things, to regular Joe people who were twittering from their phones and saying "Hey, I am going into this event." Social media was a HUGE part of this event.

Brent Leary: We are focused on small business, helping them understand the social impact of these tools and technologies. From your perspective, what are some of the key things that small business people can take out of the experiences you had while you were out at the conference?

James Andrews: I think out of the conference and out of Barack's social media strategy, I would say the ability for a small business to dare to be different and to not be stuck on what they think are the rules of engagement. The beautiful thing about Twitter is it was designed as a technology and it's in the middle of creating its own usage for different people. How Zappos is using Twitter is totally different then how the pizzeria that's really progressive in Minnesota is using Twitter. I think that for small businesses, I know this may sound crazy, but I think the best opportunity for them is to really think about not being afraid to use the technology in new and innovative ways.

I think what Twitter, social media and web 2.0 does for a brand, whether it's Barack Obama or Zappos or Rick Sanchez, who last night on CNN utilized Twitter throughout his broadcast to talk about Gustav, sends out cultural cues. It sends out the message that you are progressive, that you are trying to reach consumers in a new way and it becomes a way of talking to your customers or your followers in a way that, to me, sends out a message that you are a part of an open social community. You are open to criticism, to feedback and that you are into a two-way dialogue, which historically has been a one-way dialogue. I think that is the message that Barack is sending by utilizing Twitter and FriendFeed. He is saying, "I don't want to just be a one-way megaphone. I want to be a two-way communicator. I want to send messages out and you to tell me and give me feedback on what I am saying." I think that is what businesses can take away from using social media. If your brand sucks, people are going to tell you.

Brent Leary: {chuckles}

James Andrews: You're saying to people, I want you to tell me that. If you are Rick Sanchez and you are on CNN looking for people to give you information that your producer is not going to give you on Hurricane Gustav.

Brent Leary: Yeah.

James Andrews: I think it's a calling card to say, I'm looking for a two-way dialogue, while historically media has been about a one-way dialogue.

Brent Leary: You mention a couple of things that I am going to plug for myself because it's funny you should mention that. I just did a couple of articles about CNN's lessons for dealing with the social customer and it was all about around how Rick Sanchez went to the Twitter community and basically didn't just say "hey, check out my newscast that is getting ready to come on CNN." He said, "Help me with the newscast about Gustav."

James Andrews: Yeah.

Brent Leary: Not only am I interested in giving you information, but I am really interested in what you guys have to say and he was sharing on the newscast that he would show his screen. Here's a tweet from one and he would talk about an interesting tweet that was and how the people were using this to share information and be a part of the newscast and not just a passive listener, but be active and be a part of it. That is so engrained in this web 2.0 social customer kind of thought. Small business people can do the exact same thing.

The other thing you mentioned and I call this the audacity of CRM, which of course is based on Barack's thought about audacity. In order to captivate people on the web, you have to come out of the box. You have to be able to think creatively and you will only be able to do that if you do a couple of things. One of those is automate some of the routine processes, automate as much as you can in terms of content creation and content distribution and then analyze the impact of the content you are creating.

You can use all of these tools that are out here and if you do those things you can be more audacious. You can take the time to think out of the box, to think about how can I captivate people's attention when I know they have so much coming at them? I need to find out of the box ways to grab their attention and keep it, so your point of being audacious, being thought provoking, doing things that aren't being done by other folks. I always like to use the SEO rapper as one of the most audacious acts I know of. Who would think about rapping about search engine optimization? But yet, this guy had over three to four hundred thousand views to this YouTube video that he did on designing code.

James Andrews: Wow

Brent Leary: It's important. I love what you just said about that. I think it's a great point for small businesses to take when it comes to, not just being happy or being involved with what Barack is doing, but look at it and how can you apply some of the moves he is making to your business, because these are some great lessons he is teaching.

James Andrews: Absolutely, it is the lessons that I talk to, whether they are Fortune 500 clients that we have or whether they are personalities or celebrities that I work with. It's really all about living everywhere. Loic Le Meur (http://loiclemeur.com), who was Seesmic, says it best, when he says that if you live in all of these places in your off-campus strategy you find yourself having to go to mainstream media less and less and the things come to you. There are opportunities that come to you. I commend whoever the guru is behind this whole Barack Obama digital strategy for embracing both the mobile market...

Brent Leary: Yeah.

James Andrews: ...and the social Web 2.0 markets. I love the fact how they are using mobile. Sure we did not get to find out who the VP was and CNN broke the story, but the fact that they are leveraging mobile and leveraged mobile this weekend and asked people to donate to Red Cross right from their phone. I think that it is amazing. That would be another part of the case study when the story is told later on.

Brent Leary: Absolutely.

James Andrews: I think that all of those things speak progressive. If people really knew what it cost to build that Obama thing, if small businesses really knew what that cost, they would totally rethink their entire advertising budgets. I can look at it and tell you how much it cost.

Brent Leary: {chuckles}

James Andrews: It's just a smart way to go, moving into 2012.

Brent Leary: Well James, this has been really great and I really appreciate you stepping in and helping me out and sharing your experiences both on the personal and the professional because they are both critically important to understanding what is going on.

James Andrews: Yeah.

Brent Leary: We really appreciate it. Before I let you go, can you tell folks where they can learn more about what you are doing, writing and talking about?

James Andrews: Oh wow, I have a number of digital touch points but the primary one is the www.KeyInfluencer.com. I also Twitter at www.Twitter.com/keyinfluencer. I have a column called GeekSexy at www.FastCompany.com in the expert blogging category. If you start from there you can find me at all the other twenty places.

 To visit James Andrews, please visit: http:// www.Twitter.com/keyinfluencer

Brent Leary: One thing that I would also like to thank you for is about a month and a half ago, you hosted a great event called the Atlanta Black Bloggers Meetup.

James Andrews: Yeah, it was in conjunction with the *Blogging While Brown* convention. I am glad that you got a chance to come out; it was great to meet you face to face. We are going to be doing a lot more of those, FastCompany has something in store for me to do that across a few cities. I will keep you posted. What we should do now is do something at the inauguration in January with you and Hill Harper, let's talk about that.

Brent Leary: Absolutely, maybe we could do a Barack 2.0 Meetup or something. Let's definitely talk about that, Thanks again. This has been great information folks, your weekly Barack 2.0 Update, see you next week.

Podcast Update #6

Going Beyond Facebook, YouTube & MySpace

When most people think of social media they think of sites like Facebook, YouTube, MySpace and a few others. These sites have millions of active members, so it makes total sense to have a presence on one or more of them. The Obama campaign has active presences on each of these sites. On Facebook, for example, he has over one million fans. He's the most followed person on Twitter.

As important as it is to get involved with the big-name social sites, there are many other lesser-known sites that can be just as important in helping you connect with the kind of people you're looking to build business relationships with. Below are a few sites the Obama used in addition to the big guys that may be able to help you as well.

Ustream.tv

Ustream is a free service that allows anyone with a webcam and Internet connection to broadcast live over the Web. While you're broadcasting, those viewing your broadcast can communicate with you via instant message -- making it a truly collaborative experience. Your live streams are also archived for on-demand viewing. Obama's campaign has close to 150 archived videos on their Ustream channel, which has been viewed more than 250,000 times -- adding up to almost 90,000 hours. Now this is a far cry from the millions of views for his videos on YouTube, but it's a quick, easy way to connect with people in real-time that is growing rapidly in popularity.

 To view Barack Obama's Ustream channel, please visit:
http://www.ustream.tv/ObamaForAmerica

FriendFeed

With a growing number of people "tweeting" on Twitter, bookmarking sites using Delicious, commenting on blogs via Disqus, and performing other random social acts, it makes it hard to keep up with all the activities and conversations. FriendFeed makes it much easier for people to see what we're doing online by allowing us to easily create a feed from the activities we perform on many of the social sites we belong to. Instead of having to go to several different sites on the Web to see what a colleague is up to, you can see it all in one location via his or her FriendFeed page. They can follow your Web "adventures" as well. The Obama campaign has been using FriendFeed to make it easier to follow his tweets, Flickr pictures, YouTube videos, and blog posts.

 To view Barack Obama's FriendFeed profile please visit:
http://friendfeed.com/barackobama

Meetup

Meetup is used by organizations, groups, and clubs to organize their in-person meetings. It's a great way to get the word out about your events to people who may have common interests and would like to participate in group activities. People get event information, view member profiles, and RSVP to attend meetings. Meetup definitely makes it easier to share information, communicate with the membership, and manage group activities. Obama has used Meetup to encourage those interested in his campaign to get together, share ideas, and work with his team.

 To view Barack Obama's Meetup profile please visit: http://barackobama.meetup.com/

Check out this week's podcast as we talk through the lessons you can take from this approach.

 Listen here: http://www.box.net/shared/static/q97j1l2cmg.mp3

 Barack 2.0 Weekly Update #6
Going Beyond Facebook, YouTube & MySpace

Brent Leary: Hello and welcome to the latest edition of the Barack 2.0 weekly update. I am Brent Leary and back with me after a little bit of a hiatus, it is the online business development guru himself, David Bullock. David, how are you doing man?

David Bullock: Brent, doing well, just fine, what is it Monday? Coming off a good weekend here.

Brent Leary: Absolutely, let me just say first off congratulations, you are a new uncle. So let me just say congratulations to you.

David Bullock: I announced it on Twitter, how's that?

Brent Leary: I am sure you got many replies.

David Bullock: You know, actually I did. I am finding that when you are using those types of networks, people come back and they say congratulations, they send well wishes and cards, it's like a big family. Social networking does work.

Brent Leary: We know who's really been really effective with this social networking thing and that's part of why we do this whole update with the whole Barack 2.0 thing. Today we are going to take a couple of minutes to talk about social networking and we are going to talk about it from a perspective, not concentrating on the big guys. We do concentrate a little bit before we get into the main topic, we do an update. Let's go ahead and do the Twitter update before we step away from the big guys.

David Bullock: All right, I'm on www.Twitterholic.com and I'm looking to see where Senator Obama is right now as far as his Twitter following and today he is at 78,860 followers and he is well over 10,000 in front of the next person who is Kevin Rose who is at 63,171. He continues to get more and more followers as the election becomes closer.

Brent Leary: Wow, I remember when we first started doing this, he was about seven or eight thousand behind Kevin Rose and now he is over 10,000 above.

David Bullock: Here is the thing that is funny, his friends listening is at 82,000, whereas, Kevin Rose is at 102. You see that he is following more people than are following him # 1. Kevin Rose has done over 1000 updates and he has only done 195.

Brent Leary: Yeah, it's almost unfair to compare him to anybody, but I do like the comparison because we did that during our webinar where we compared how the Obama campaign approached Twitter, as opposed to Senator Clinton and I think she was along the same lines as followers although she didn't follow anybody.

David Bullock: Right.

Brent Leary: I guess it's that philosophy, you follow me, I'll follow you, I might not read everything but I will do you the courtesy of following you.

David Bullock: That part is the reciprocation part, it's mutual – a two way street now. That is what you are looking for more then anything else. The part that really makes the fact that Senator Obama is doing more is that he is spread out on other media. He is giving updates on television, radio, the newspaper and other social networking sites that we are going to talk about in a minute. Whereas, if you are just online then your reach can only go so far, people do not live online, they live in the real world.

Brent Leary: Absolutely.

David Bullock: The matrix does not have everyone so to speak.

Brent Leary: {chuckles} Not everybody took the blue pill, is that it?

David Bullock: Mmhmm

Brent Leary: It's really important, you said a couple of things, now he is on television and he has access to media outlets that none of us can imagine to have, but he doesn't stop at that. This is why we wanted to concentrate on the other things that he is doing and the other sites he is using that doesn't get the headlines, like the Facebook or a YouTube. In fact, I wrote something recently for Inc. magazine called *Going Beyond Facebook, YouTube and Twitter* and it was based on some of the other social sites that the Obama campaign is using and taking full advantage of that small business people we can be doing the same things.   We know about how he used YouTube, he has his own YouTube channel and he has numbers of videos out there and they get millions of views. He was already on YouTube, he doesn't have to do anything else, but he is also using something else called UStream. David, maybe you want to fill folks in on what

UStream is and why it's another viable option for not only Obama's campaign to use but for small business people to use?

 Read Brent's article *Going Beyond Facebook, YouTube and Twitter* here: http://technology.inc.com/internet/articles/200809/leary.html

David Bullock: UStream is a free service that actually allows you to almost own your own television station online. That's the analogy I would like to make. You are using your webcam and an internet connection to broadcast all over the web. The nice thing is that people can see you and when they see you – it's almost as if you become a celebrity in their mind and they can get to know you. You can deliver information streaming free using www.UStream.tv. You can go ahead and create your own channel. You can do webinars. You can push your audio out, your video out. You can invite people to meet you there. You can sit there and say, I am doing a broadcast for and essentially you are your own television and production station and it's done with the technologies that you have right there on your computer along with a webcam. The internet has created a situation where the little guy – the small business can have the capability that once was only afforded to some of the bigger production companies.

> ### Live Streaming Video
>
> All You need are the right Tools To Connect With Your Market
>
> **Audio Editing Tool:**
> http://audacity.sourceforge.net/
>
> **Podcasting:**
> http://www.blogtalkradio.com/
> http://www.hipcast.com/
>
> **Video Capture Tools:**
> Flip Camera - www.theflip.com
> Computer WebCam - www.logitech.com
>
> **Video Capture Software:**
> www.Camtasia.com
> www.techsmith.com/camtasia.asp
> www.microsoft.com/windowsxp/downloads/updates/moviemaker2.mspx
> www.JingProject.com

Brent Leary: Yeah and the cool thing about it is it's live streamed. I was actually checking out something yesterday. Somebody put out a tweet that said, hey I am live streaming right now, join me and so I went there, I clicked on it and he is just sitting in front of his computer and he is talking and doing some things. It was somewhat boring what he was doing but the mere fact that you can use these things in combination. If you have a couple of hundred of people following you a Twitter, you can put out a tweet that says, check me out on my live stream and people can click on it and see you and they can interact with you. If you have something interesting that you are talking about or you are sharing information, this is a way to do it and get instant real time feedback collaboration. That's a little different if you load up something on YouTube, because you don't get real time interaction, but it's still a great vehicle, but you can get real time collaborative interaction experiences with people so that you can grab them right there and how much does it cost to do that David?

David Bullock: It's free and that's the part that's interesting. You said something there, whatever the guy was doing there was boring, now let's think about this for a minute, he was online, streaming in that moment and he was boring. This means that if you are actually interesting, people will be interested and you can create your own news in the marketplace. If you put it out there and you capture it, you can then take that capture and put that up on YouTube.

Brent Leary: Absolutely.

David Bullock: You take that capture and you start using that as a viral video. If it is interesting, it gives good information, good content within the context of people wanting to know about something, you have something that you can use repeatedly as a promotional piece.

Brent Leary: That's one of the hidden networks, not really hidden, but not really known to enough people.

David Bullock: They are not headliners.

Brent Leary: Right, they are like the off Broadway kind of folks here. But we need to know about them as small business people.

David Bullock: But as we know, off Broadway does make a lot of money.

Brent Leary: They wouldn't be off Broadway or continue to be off Broadway if they weren't making money, because they would just be out of business.

David Bullock: Exactly.

Brent Leary: Let's talk about another one that is really well known in the geek-dom that you and I are probably a part of. Typically, small business people have not heard of FriendFeed. They've heard of Twitter and Twitter is a great utility. FriendFeed is another interesting one that more and more people are starting to take notice of. David, maybe you could fill them in on what FriendFeed is and why Obama's team is using it.

David Bullock: FriendFeed allows the user to aggregate or get all of these streams. You have Twitter, YouTube, and Flickr – all of the places where people are putting information up and you want to follow them. FriendFeed allows you to put those all into one place. You can look in one place to see what people are doing and to see what they are posting. You can follow people and keep up with them from one place as opposed to going into multiple places.

Notice what is happening here in the marketplace. You had all of these individual situations like Flickr, which was picture sharing. You have YouTube, which is video sharing; you have Twitter, which is a micro blogging platform. These three are all very different, but FriendFeed ties them all together. You have a situation there where you are starting to get an aggregation and combination so that you can see what's going on across multiple platforms from one place. Which means they are becoming more convenient to you as a business owner to be everywhere in communication with more people without having to be in a frenzy over it.

Brent Leary: Yeah, I am like this. FriendFeed is important because if you are creating content through these different vehicles and channels and social sites, it becomes hard to keep up with all the conversations you are involved in. Being able to use something like FriendFeed, which will basically aggregate all of the stuff that you are doing so that your tweets from Twitter or your comments from something like Disqus, your pictures in Flickr, your videos from YouTube. They are all of these dispersed areas, but if people really want to keep track of what you are doing, you have to make it as easy as possible if you can.

David Bullock: The ease of use is key.

Brent Leary: Yeah, so FriendFeed allows you to aggregate all of the stuff that you are doing on the web so that the people who want to know what you are doing can find it easily. Then they can interact with you from FriendFeed, they can actually comment on stuff that you do on other sites, they can comment right on FriendFeed and you can see the conversation as it takes place in one location.   Great stuff.

So we have done UStream, we have done FriendFeed. The next one we want to talk about is MeetUp. MeetUp is a great site that allows you to get all of your online activities together for putting on collaborative experiences and being able to set up organizations and being able to set up real meetings and do it all online, so you actually have a better experience at the actual real meeting in person...

David Bullock: Which is offline. This is the most important part of this; one of the things that we talked about earlier was that when you have someone online, the key to developing a real relationship with someone is to pull them offline. The www.MeetUp.com allows you to organize and/or find groups that you can actually meet. Imagine if you are a business owner, you are looking for clients, and you have a particular area of expertise – you can find people who already may be meeting about that thing that you want to talk to them about.

Brent Leary: Yeah, absolutely. The thing about it is we do our networking events and one of the things that I came back from a conference where I spoke, but the coolest part about it is I actually met people that I had been tweeting, emailing and commenting on blogs for months. It was so nice to be able to meet them but already have a story behind it. You felt like you already knew these people. It enhanced the actual experience of the face-to-face meeting. That's what I think all of these tools can do. They should be used in combination. You can't really cut off your face-to-face networking just because you are great online, they work too well together. You should be pulling them together and MeetUp is a great example of how you can do that.

Meeting Face-to-Face

What is Meetup.com?

Taking the internet off the internet. Meeting with people offline is the best way to develop meaningful relationships.

Don't use technology to hide from your customers.

Use techology to connect with your market.

Meetup.com allows you to organize and schedule offline meetings.

David Bullock: It's a collaboration tool. I am going to Blog World Expo - I am speaking there at the end of this week. Already, I am getting these tweets, let's exchange cell phone numbers so we can have lunch, or let's make sure that we meet up while we are there. You should be using your online tools as a networking augmentation situation to refine and develop the relationship offline – or one on one. The online space if you really look at it, lets you go from one to many in one shot.

Brent Leary: Right.

David Bullock: It allows people to decide to interact with you. Once they decide to interact with you, once again you have to be interesting and interested enough in what they are doing to develop a real relationship, because only through the real relationship can the real business, the exchange, or the transaction actually occur.

Brent Leary: This is just great stuff, great lessons once again as the whole process goes along. We have learned and we learn as much as the people who listen about how we can literally use all of these different tools in a real strategy to engage people not just online but to cross the line into reality – actually meeting people and going even further. That's how you solidify the relationship. It may start online, but at some point, to really make it hum, it makes so much more sense to get face to face and these are the kinds of tools that will put you face to face with the right kind of people. That's the important thing. FriendFeed, UStream and MeetUp are free tools to use. There are thousands, if not hundred of thousands of people already on them that you can connect with. Once again, look at how the Obama campaign has used these tools effectively to build the ground game that they have built.

David Bullock: I just want to reiterate, these tools are available to you free online. The key is to developing – or get with people- Brent and I are using these tools every day to move forward and to network and to create more business out of nothing. It starts with a conversation. It starts with communication, which then moves to collaboration. It's available to you. You just have to find people that know how to use it effectively. This is the guide – the blueprint and you are seeing it play out on a national scale right now with Senator Obama's campaign.

Brent Leary: Let us ask you, because we will be putting this up so people can comment on what is going on. Tell us about some sites that you think are great that you are using that maybe the rest of us can benefit from.

David Bullock: Exactly, the blog is there because we can't know everything – nor can we be everywhere. You may know of this great site, because new sites are appearing online everyday. So as we move along here, the headliners are always going to be in the news, but the ones that might be the most effective may never be reported about. We want to know about those too.

Brent Leary: This has been your Barack 2.0 weekly update, we'll be back next week, but once again, we need your comments, we need your feedback, visit www.Barack20.com, check it out. See you next week.

Podcast Update #7

Practicing What He Preaches

As this site is closing in on its two-month birthday, and this being the seventh weekly update, we thought we'd take a few minutes to touch on how we've been using the social media lessons being taught by Senator Obama's campaign. It's important to us for you to know that we're learning along with you, and that we are putting these strategies to use with this site. We touch on how this series got started with an online article, a conversation, a PowerPoint presentation and a webinar. It then turned into a website and weekly podcast. We've tweeted about it, and created content in different forms - text, audio and video. We've shared it with people in our social networks - both online and offline.

To keep you informed and ourselves honest, we talk through some stats that let you know how successful we've been to date in reaching people by using the Barack 2.0 lessons covered on this site. While you listen to this week's update, you may want to keep your eyes on the diagram below, as we use this to talk about some specific stats:

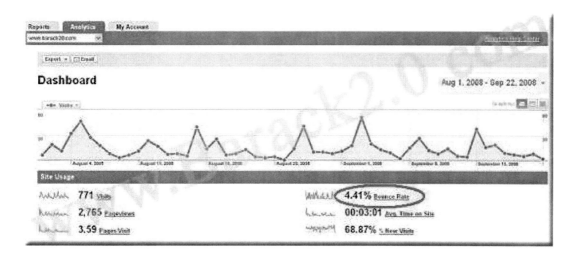

As always, we welcome your thoughts and observations. Any feedback you can provide to the B2.0 community is greatly appreciated!

Check out this week's podcast as we talk through the lessons you can take from this approach.

Listen here: http://www.box.net/shared/static/pu3593y56b.mp3

 Barack 2.0 Weekly Update #7
Practicing What He Preaches

Brent Leary: Hello and welcome to this week's Barack 2.0 weekly update. I am Brent Leary and as always I have with me the online business development guru extraordinaire Mr. David Bullock. How are you doing?

David Bullock: Yes, Sir. Good afternoon, how are you?

Brent Leary: I'm doing fine and I'm glad that you are able to be with me today after the big weekend. You were at Blog World Expo dropping a little knowledge on the folks.

David Bullock: Blog World Expo was great. I think it was at two thousand people, that was the roll there.

Brent Leary: Wow.

David Bullock: Yeah, bloggers, all the social media folks were there. There are bunches of new tools, many new developments in the marketplace. It's a very exciting time for podcasting, blogging, content generation, sharing. The market is really moving fast, I really enjoyed it.

Brent Leary: I have already received some feedback that you just knocked it out that park, so I am not going to add too much to that except that is what I expect from you.

David Bullock: All right, I appreciate it.

Brent Leary: Let's move on because we don't have a lot of time this week, but we have a special show for the folks to talk a little bit about something. How this Barack 2.0 thing is moving. Before we get into that, we do this weekly update to see where Barack Obama, how many followers he has on Twitter. So if you would please give us the latest number.

David Bullock: If you go over to www.TwitterHolic.com as of today, the 22nd of September, 2008, you will find that Barack Obama had 82, 598 followers at this time. He has eclipsed Kevin Rose, who is in the second position who is at 64,000. He is pulling away quickly. I suspect that Barack Obama will be the first one to hit the hundred thousand followers on Twitter. We are probably about forty days out from the election at this time, so it would be something if he actually got that that 100,000 showing interest in him and his message. And/or not even his message but just showing interest. What you have to look at is Twitter is who is interested in listening to what you have to say. Not all these people may be Democrats; they may be people world wide just wanting to see just what is he talking about. What is he tweeting about on a day-to-day basis?

Brent Leary: Yeah, wouldn't it be interesting to see if they had a demographic or geographic breakdown of where people are following him from, that would be cool.

David Bullock: Absolutely, when you look at Twitter from a business side, it is an opportunity to build a list. These people have opted in to follow you voluntarily and they can opt out at any given time. They do not give you any notice, but if you are keeping them interested and you are interesting, things will continue to move forward. Barack is doing an excellent job there.

Brent Leary: You gave me a chance to look at your slides and it was great. There seems to be a lot of interest in just what we have done and by looking at what the Barack Obama campaign has done with social media and what started out for us with an article and a PowerPoint presentation and turned into a webinar and a website.

There is a great story in just what we have done by looking at what they have done by way of using social media. You did such a great job with your slides. Maybe you could walk folks through what we have done and what is leading to some nice traffic on the web.

David Bullock: Let's take a step back and look at the foundation of what we have done here. With any business or anything that you start out with there is an idea. There is a story in the greater marketplace around Obama and what he was doing and how he was using social media. That was the underlying story that Brent and I saw and said, that is a good story but no one is covering this from the business aspect. Everyone is looking at it from the political side of how we are going to do this and up against the republicans. That's all well and good, but how can you use this from a business standpoint? That was the underlying story because you have to look at the market story, which is always there. There is a story of the visitor that is coming to the site, but Brent and I have our story and we are going to put our particular spin on it. That is what led to the initial buoyancy of the idea.

Brent Leary: Good stuff and what you said was right. We basically are doing the same thing that everybody out there is doing, with an idea. We created an article – content and put it out on the web and got feedback. That feedback prompted us to discuss, maybe we should do so more stuff around this. We did a webinar – which is something that anybody can do. To talk about some of the things that we saw in terms of the campaign and how they used social media and how small business people can use it. We got great feedback from that, which again, is one of those web things – you can get that instantaneous feedback. When we looked at the feedback we said, "Maybe we should do something like put a little blog site together. Maybe we'll be able to do some quick easy updates that take different looks and feels of what's going on and how they are using Twitter or how they are using some other service and how it is impacting the way they are able to communicate with people they are trying to engage with."

All of these are little things that any small businessperson can do with the tools that are out there. If they think about how they can captivate the audience, they are trying to get with the content they can create.

David Bullock: Again, it goes back to starting with that interesting story. The story was in the marketplace. Barack Obama is running for this position. Look at the underdog story here. How is he going to make that happen and low and behold he was using technology that small business owners have at their fingertips. They can use it now, which makes it more appealing because you can do it too. It's a "Yes, We Can" situation which is the underlying message here.

Brent Leary: One of the things that you mentioned that got a lot of interesting feedback when you were doing your presentation, what do you call it? The bounce rate...

David Bullock: Oh, the bounce rate.

Brent Leary: Yeah, could you explain what the bounce rate is and explain what bounce rate we are getting on the site and how that has piqued some people's interest?

David Bullock: Bounce rate briefly is this. When someone comes to a website and they don't find what they want, they leave. That is really what it comes down to. You are not interesting, they are not interested and they bounce out. That is what bounce rate is. How long they stay on the site and do they continue forward to second or third page.   Now, a good bounce rate typically is like 30%, typical bounce rate is somewhere between 50-70%.

On the www.Barack20.com site right now, our bounce rate is 4.14% since the site started on August 1st until September 22, 2008, which means the traffic is extremely targeted. It is interested in what we have. We are interesting to them and they are coming in and looking at an average of 3.59 pages, which means people are not just coming to the site and seeing one page, they are coming in and looking around to listen to the podcast, read the posts, see what other interesting things we have on the site. The average person is staying on the site for three minutes, which means they are probably listening to one of the updates before they download it. Here is the kicker, we have upwards of 70% of the people coming to the site are new people, which means these are people that have never heard of us before and have never been to the site before and they are coming to see what it is all about.

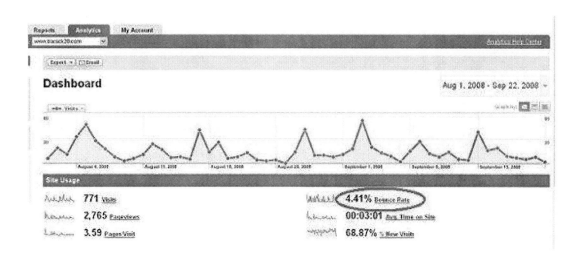

Brent Leary: That's what it is all about. When you mention that bounce rate thing, that stuck out to me because what you are saying is the kind of content that we are putting out for Barack 2.0, the people that come to the site that is what they are looking for apparently and they are downloading, listening or something. That lets us know what we are putting out there is of interest to the people that are looking for this kind of stuff.

David Bullock: One of the things that we are also doing which is a little different and I was called on it this weekend. "You are not collecting any names." We are not coercing people; if you give us your email address then we will give you this.

Brent Leary and David Bullock

Brent Leary: {chuckles}

David Bullock: We've had close to 900 downloads. The people have come and engaged with us, almost 1000 times within the last 45 some odd days, voluntarily. That is a very key point. We are not trading the email address or the possibility of communicating with you again for the actual content because the context for the *Barack 2.0: Barack Obama's Social Media Business Lessons* is strong enough to bring people back repeatedly.

Brent Leary: That is what we are looking for folks. These lessons are for you to look at. Not just how they are using social media but how you could potentially use it for yourself. That is what these lessons are about and we are glad that when you do find us, that you are finding something of substance, at least enough to download or listen and we really appreciate it. We also appreciate any kind of feedback that you can provide us.

David Bullock: Comments, we want comments. We want to know what you're thinking. As we get into short strokes now and getting closer and closer to the election, you may see some different things. Phone calls, how is that accounted for? What are you seeing on the television and radio? You are out there looking at it. Assess how it is working. Is it effective? What is his message? Is it changing? Those are things that everybody has an opinion on, it's affecting them differently, and we would like to know what you think.

Brent Leary: We did a little bit different update this week, but we wanted to do this because we wanted to let you know that we are eating our own dog food. Everything that we talk about as we look at the Barack Obama campaign and their social media strategy, we are learning too and we are putting it to use.

David Bullock: As you look at the small business lessons for small business, using social media. Look at what we did, the webinar, we have created the podcast, we have created downloads, we have the site up, it is being linked, we are getting spidered, we are getting business, we are getting downloads. These are all things that you can do right now, it's all available to you and we are giving it to you in small bite sized chunks so you don't have to do it all in one day.

Brent Leary: This has been another Barack 2.0 Weekly update. We will be back next week with another one. Folks, we will have something special for you, but you need to continue to listen. Again, we can't overstate this enough, give us your comments, your feedback, because we want to be sure that we are touching on the things that you want to hear about.   This has been another Barack 2.0 weekly update. See you next week.

Podcast Update #8

Going Viral with User Generated Content

If you can find captivating ways to express your ideas to the world, the world will help you spread that vision in ways you may never have dreamed of. If you share your vision with the world, the world may help bring perspective to it, and make it better.

This week we look at how the Obama campaign embraced the above philosophy and create an environment where people, inspired by their message, invested their own time and money to create compelling content that literally has reached millions of people. Content that extends the ideas and vision put forth by the campaign, but powered by the creativity of individuals inspired by the original idea.

We look at the following for examples of user-generated content inspired by the ideals of the Obama campaign and how they have worked as unofficial surrogate: www.Dipdive.com in relation to the release of the *Yes We Can - Voices of a Grassroots Movement* CD project.

Millions Inspired by
Senator Barack Obama...

"YES WE CAN"

To visit Dipdive.com go to – http://www.Dipdive.com
Or the sister site http://www.HopeActChange.com

See Addendum – Figure Web 1.22 and 1.23

As you will hear, these are a few interesting examples of how great ideas, expressed in captivating ways, can inspire people to help us spread our message. Now these examples are on a much broader scale and scope than any small business could really expect to function on. We really don't need this scale in order to find success with these strategies. Great comments left on blogs are examples of effective impact user-generated content. Tweets from customers can be generated content as well. The thing to remember is to concentrate on sharing your ideas and vision in ways that move people to act - on your behalf.

Listen here: http://www.box.net/shared/static/lhrrioujdm.mp3

 Barack 2.0 Weekly Update #8
Going Viral with User Generated Content

Brent Leary: Hello and welcome to this week's Barack 2.0 Weekly Update, I am Brent Leary. As always, I have with me, the man, the myth, the legend, David Bullock.

David Bullock: Brent, I am fine this afternoon. How are you?

Brent Leary: Well, I am just trying to find a gallon of gas.

David Bullock: We are having some significant things here. Nashville is in the same situation, gas is scarce here. Something is really going on with our supply here in the south, I'll tell you.

Brent Leary: {chuckles} Well look folks, we are going to talk about a couple of things here, we are going to try to keep it to five or seven minutes, some times we just have to go overboard. One of the things we always do is to get a weekly update on how many people are following Barack Obama on Twitter. David, if you could tell us what that is.

David Bullock: Now, on the 29th of September 2008, Barack Obama is at 87,932 followers. He is the number one spot above the second person who only has 65 thousand, listen to me, *only* has, 65,184 which is now well over 20,000 lead over the next person. Barack is putting on somewhere between 300-500 people a day as followers on Twitter. Again, if we thought that Twitter was not an important communication factor in this election, we were wrong. We will talk a little bit more about how it becomes more important as we move along.

Brent Leary: Absolutely and really, we are going to touch on something that Twitter did around the debate that was fascinating, but before we do that, I know something that caught your attention David, was this www.Dipdive.com.

David Bullock: Right, www.DipDive.com is a site that is a video playing site – music videos and that type of thing but it's at www.DipDive.com. If you go there, there is a video there that I had not seen before that had escaped me, but it's "Yes, We Can." What it seems like is one of the musicians and writers from the Black Eyed Peas went ahead and took the "Yes, We Can" speech that Barack Obama did and actually did a musical montage against that speech. It was very viral, has been viewed by well over a million people at this point. We know that music, as well as video are extremely viral. In fact, I am looking at the number of people that have seen this so far; 4.5 million people have dipped – pushed against this video. If we look at this from a business perspective, we all know that if you have a good jingle with your business or associated with your business, everyone has their own theme song so to speak. If you can get that now and push that out online, it has the possibility of going viral. If that is the case, you will get that much more exposure. Obviously, that is what has happened with this video here.

Brent Leary: I remember when this video first came out. I want to say at least seven or eight months ago. When I heard about it – I heard about it from people – at least ten different people sent me emails and says "Hey, you have got to check this video out" and they know I am not really into politics. It is going to change the way you view politics. It's going to capture your attention, just check it out.   I was like, okay. People are saying that, I am going to do it. Of course, it was a very interesting video. It was visceral. One thing that is interesting that I wanted to point out. On YouTube, the same video has been viewed close to ten million times.

David Bullock: Wow

Brent Leary: And it was added eight months ago, but what you are saying is on DipDive, which is a totally separate thing, it is a site unto itself. They have four million dips, as they call it. When you add these things up…

David Bullock: That's a lot of exposure.

Brent Leary: Yeah, that's thirteen millions views to this thing. That is unbelievable. How much did that cost Obama? Nothing

David Bullock: Nothing and that's the part which is so interesting here. When you have a story – we all, as business owners, have word of mouth. We are always looking for advocates in the marketplace that say that we are so good at what we do that we are going to go out and tell people. What if you did such a good job for one of your clients that they did a video and said, this is how good this is? That word of mouth advertising, or take a step back, instead of them doing it, what if you took a video camera, which is very easy these days, or recorded them talking about your business and you made the montage. You put it out there and it went viral. That is the same type of situation you can create for your business.

Brent Leary: This is an exaggerated example of user-generated content.

David Bullock: Mmhmm

Brent Leary: Because, once again, Barack and his team didn't have anything to do with this, I don't think. I think this is all about Will.i.am and him getting together his friends and they created this video. That's an exaggerated version of this, but user generated content is something that we could also put into play because we know people. We may have some customers that really like us and maybe we can get them to do a testimonial for us. There are other ways that you can get this kind of content that you don't necessarily have to pay for, but can work for you. As David said, it becomes viral. Yeah, it would be nice to have 13 million views…

David Bullock: Right

Brent Leary: But we don't necessarily need that much of the viral effect.

David Bullock: No, if you look at it, just from a very simplistic standpoint – a comment on a blog is user generated content.

Brent Leary: Absolutely.

David Bullock: A comment in a forum is user generated content. The email that someone writes to you saying that you have done a great job or this is how your service worked for me, that is user generated content. The question is, start looking at that content and how you can repurpose it to actually achieve your aims.

Brent Leary: Absolutely. One other thing, since we are sort of digging into this whole content thing and it's user generated content. There is another grassroots effort, I guess is a way you can put it, called *Voices Of A Grassroots Movement*, which is all of these different artists, who come together to create a CD of music – 18 song CD - from people like Stevie Wonder and Sheryl Crow.

David Bullock: Yolanda Adams, they are all here.

Brent Leary: There are all there. They all donated a song to this CD that is called Yes, We Can and you can go to the www.BarackObama.com site and get it. What it is, I forget what the actual cost is, but whatever you pay is a donation to the Barack Obama campaign. Once again, this is user generated content and it is being used to build some donations for the campaign.   Once again, think creatively about how you can engage the people around you to maybe help you do some content, or help them to do the content, which will in turn help you draw some attention and credibility to your web presence.

   See Addendum – Figure Web 1.23

David Bullock: I was looking here at the *Yes, We Can: Voices of a Grassroots Movement* website and I was looking down at the bottom here. Under the press content it says downloads, you can download the album cover. You can download the press release, but more importantly, you can download a flyer and pass to your friends. Notice something, download flyer you can print – they tell you what to do and pass to your friends.

Brent Leary: Absolutely

David Bullock: They are actually giving you a way to push this offline from a website. Right below it, embed this player on your site. They are giving you a way to put this on your site so that you can tell everybody about it. Look at this, they are helping it go viral by giving you exact instructions and giving you the tools to do so.

   See Addendum – Figure Web 1.24

Brent Leary: One other thing that we will tie into this, we are not going to get into the politics of the debate, but one of the things that we looked at and thought was really interesting as the debate was taking place.

On September 25, 2008, Twitter put up a new site called, www.election.Twitter.com. As the debate was going on you could follow the tweets in real time that related to the debate. Once again, this may be a little far out there, but this is user generated content too. Anytime you are able to do something and you are able to get people to talk about it, hopefully they are talking about it positively, but if you can get them to talk about it and you can actually use those conversations as content for you to promote your business and your website, do it. There is absolutely no reason why you shouldn't do it.

David Bullock: We are looking here; notice that Twitter tweets as they call them on Twitter, can actually get search engine traffic. You can direct people where you want to go. If you entered into this conversation where something that got these people's attention, because many people here looking at this stream. If you entered this conversation with something that was close enough to it to get their attention, for lack of a better term, redirect some of this traffic to anything you wanted them to go to at this point.

Brent Leary: I think it's just critically important to understand, somebody was mentioning this to me, I think they were involved in tracking and how search is being done, a report I had found. The fastest growing area in search is not on Google searches, it's on social media searches.

David Bullock: Mmhmm

Brent Leary: People are always going to be looking to media for searching things. To get real time conversation and real time research intelligence, you can be doing searches in something like Twitter where conversations are always going on and you can find out what is really the latest and greatest in your industry by doing a search not only in Google, but also searching within things like Twitter.

David Bullock: Well Twitter and Technorati, the engines in the blogosphere so to speak – it's real time. There is someone always talking about something in that particular social media space. Now, if you need to know something and you are involved with the community, you can quickly ask the community and you'll get answers. The idea of going to one place or one entity controlling all of the information, that idea I believe is long gone.

Brent Leary: Yeah, I think it went with the treasury secretary trying to do that whole $700 Billion and just let him control all the money, that didn't happen.

David Bullock: Well, we aren't going to talk about that.

Brent Leary: We aren't going to talk about that, but this is really important. We actually went over the time we said we would because this is a lot of good information. This has been your Barack 2.0 weekly update, but before we let you go away, we do want to invite you to share the stories that you had, maybe some success stories about how you are utilizing social media in your strategy or as I like to say, win friends and influence people. It's really important for us to hear from you. David, tell them, if they do share their stories and we like them, tell them how we may help them out.

David Bullock: If you give us a story that really shows the utilization of social media for business purposes, what we would like to do is bring you on the show and we will interview you. That gives you and your business much more exposure to the people we are exposing the Barack 2.0 concept. Meaning, how can we do a case study with you, using social media for your business. We would love to highlight you and show the world that this stuff really does work, if you know what you are doing, you get the right instructions and then you take action.

Brent Leary and David Bullock

Podcast Update #9

A Conversation with the Tech Team Behind BarackObama.com

This week is a different kind of update. As host of Technology For Business Sake (TFBS) I have the great pleasure of having excellent guests on with me to discuss how technology can help small businesses compete, thrive and survive in a "web-enhanced" world.

Recently I had the opportunity to speak with Jascha Franklin-Hodge, co-founder and chief technology of Blue State Digital. Blue State Digital is the technology partner the Obama campaign turned to build and manage their web presence. This includes the creation of the Blue State Digital powered sites www.BarackObama.com, and the social networking component www.My.BarackObama.com. These sites have been responsible for:

- Capturing 1.4M email addresses

- Creating over 1M user accounts

- Promoting over 75,000 campaign events

- Supporting donation efforts that helped raise over $250M

Jascha shares how Blue State Digital started with the campaign and built the www.BarackObama.com site in less than a week, the strategy behind the campaign's web presence and the way it has fostered a wildly active community. He also discusses what small businesses can take away from the campaign with respect to using technology to engage people. Please enjoy this TFBS "re-broadcast"!

Visit Jascha Franklin-Hodge and Blue State Digital at: http://www.bluestatedigital.com/

Check out this week's podcast as we talk through the lessons you can take from this approach.

Listen here: http://www.box.net/shared/static/fps1a0ix79.mp3

Barack 2.0 Weekly Update #9
A Conversation with the Tech Team Behind BarackObama.com

It's time now for this edition of Technology for Business $ake, brought to you by the maker of the award-winning Blackberry devices, Research in Motion. Get ready to learn how your small business can utilize technology to be more productive and profitable. Let's get started. Here are your hosts, Brent Leary and Michael Thomas.

Brent Leary: Welcome back to Technology for Business $ake. It is my pleasure to announce my next guest, the co-founder and chief technology officer for Blue State Digital, Jascha Franklin-Hodge. Jascha, thank you for joining me today.

Jascha Franklin-Hodge: Hey, my pleasure.

Brent Leary: Now, some people may not be familiar with the name of your company, Blue State Digital, but they are probably familiar with one of your clients and particularly one of the clients in the way they have used the web to put their name out there. The website is www.BarackObama.com and you guys are the technology force behind the scenes.

Jascha Franklin-Hodge: Mmhmm

Brent Leary: Tell us a little bit about Blue State Digital and how you got started. Lead us up to the point where you started working with the Barack Obama campaign.

Jascha Franklin-Hodge: Absolutely. The company actually came out of Howard Dean's presidential campaign originally. I and some of the other co-founders were working on his internet team and when the campaign ended, I think one of the takeaways that many people both inside and outside the campaign had is that there are many things that we didn't quite get right. One thing that we really excelled at online was our ability to engage people to tap into their enthusiasm, their energy to fundraise, to get them to go out and knock on doors, to make phone calls and write letters.

We started a company that was geared around the idea of bringing those capabilities, both at a technical level and at a strategic level to other campaigns and other candidates who wouldn't necessarily have the resources to do it otherwise. We have created a suite of software that incorporates CRM functionality, but is really geared around getting people engaged online, around a cause or an issue - getting them not only to talk with the organization. Whether it is a campaign, a political campaign, a non-profit group or an advocacy group, engaged with each other as well, to form groups and getting them to discuss the issues on blogs, create their own content and have their own events. In many ways, I think that is the secret sauce of what we do; both with our toolset and with the strategy that we provide. We help these organizations tap into the power and enthusiasm of their supporters and put that to good use in a way that can only be done with the internet as the medium for that interaction.

We have been in business since 2004. In very early 2007 the Obama exploratory committee approached us and said "Hey, we are going to be making a run here and we really like what you guys are doing and the approach that you are taking." With about a week's notice we got a website up and running for Barack Obama that has this rich social functionality, as well as the standard stuff that you are going to need in a campaign: fundraising, emailing sign-ups and all of

---

Brent Leary and David Bullock

that kind of stuff. We launched this on the day that he announced his candidacy and we have been with the campaign ever since.

It's been a really amazing experience for us because what we have seen is a campaign that has really embraced, not just the technology, as this is a great way to raise money, but the technology and the program that can be built around it as a way to really have a more meaningful interaction with supporters and voters. This is a campaign that has had now over 150,000 events around the country that have been scheduled but the vast majority of those weren't official campaign events. These were events where people who were encouraged by the campaign to have a house party or debate watch party or go and hand out stickers at a local neighborhood event. These were events that these people created on their own and other folks found them and signed up. That is just one example but what this campaign has really embraced that power of these tools and this technology to connect people to each other in order to organize and get active on behalf of the campaign.

Brent Leary: When they initially approached you, did they already have a pretty well thought out internet strategy and say, "Hey, we need this, can you guys do it?" Or was it a combination of what can we do with the web?

Jascha Franklin-Hodge: It was definitely a combination of that. I think that they understood and what was really thought out from the get-go and I think my sense comes from the candidate is an understanding of the power of engagement. This is a guy who was a community organizer with the power of giving people a sense that they can have a role, that they can make a difference. I think when the campaign looked at the internet strategy, they said "We recognize that this technology can make this possible, but we are not 100% sure on all of the ways in which it might work." They came to us because we had an existing toolset that was well suited to this kind of individual empowerment – via group empowerment – via the web.

It's really been an ongoing process, working with them over the past 19 months now, to develop the details of that. We have done a lot of new functionality. We have tweaked a lot of things that we already had and it's a mix. They have some tremendously smart people working at the campaign trying to navigate this and figure out what is the right internet strategy. We are there to be their support system and actually build the things that need to get built. But it has been a real collaboration and one that I am extremely grateful to have had the opportunity to do and very proud of the results.

Brent Leary: You mentioned earlier that you guys really cut your teeth on the Howard Dean campaign when you were mixing internet strategy and politics. What has changed? That was about 2004 or maybe even before that. What has changed now? A lot has changed. What were the important changes that have made this campaign and the way that they use technologies so much larger as opposed to what it was? Howard Dean was successful; I didn't want to say that he wasn't. That is why I said "how much more larger and how much more impact has it made the difference in technology from then to now?" How has that played the role in what's happened here?

Jascha Franklin-Hodge: That's a good question. I think that some of it's just been the natural evolution of the online space. There are more people online now. There is more use of social media within the online realm, whether it is social networking tools, where people are publishing the details of their life to their friends and family, whether it is blogging or YouTube video. There is a much greater understanding across the internet and across the nation that these tools are not just another pathway for traditional publishers to give you their content; that these tools are actually a way for people to participate in the content making process and to have their own voice, network and community.

I think that some of what we have been able to take advantage of that natural growth in the online space and in that sense of online engagement and community. There has also been a growing recognition within the political world that the way that you need to run an online campaign isn't the way that offline campaigns have traditionally been run. Traditionally campaigns are very top-down organizations. Somebody at the top sets the strategy and it trickles down through the organization and there are very clear lines of hierarchy and very clear and strict reporting matrix and all of this. While that stuff continues to exist and is an important piece of campaign organization, there is another piece that can exist when you actually let go of some of the control that campaigns that have traditionally existed on.

When you say to people, even four years ago, to go to a campaign and say to them, "you should have a blog on your website, but not just your blog, but you should let your supporters have a blog on your website." The idea was just … "What if they say things that aren't on message? What is going to happen when we open that up?" I think that what has happened, as people have seen this done and as there has been some success stories coming out of this, people have realized that the only way this works is if you let go of some of that control.

The media has come along as well; there was a time if somebody made an offensive comment on a blog post on your site, people would report on it as though you had said it yourself. I think there is a much better understanding how to cover social media and how to cover these types of online sites. I think that those factors have played in and at the end of the day, what it really came down to was having a campaign that truly embraced the concept of supporter empowerment, not just as a means of getting people to give money, or to cast their vote, but to real vibrant and critical part of their organizing strategy.

We have a candidate who understands and embraces that and technology that we have that makes it possible to really tap into that potential. I think what we have seen in the Obama campaign is this explosion that is beyond anything that has been done in online politics, in terms of whether you are measuring by number of people who are working on the site or the size of emails lists, dollars raised, events held or groups organized. All of these things have been off the charts in this campaign and it is that synergy between an organization that really gets it and a set of a technology that really makes it possible.

Brent Leary: That's interesting because everything that you just said can absolutely apply to business and how businesses use social media. It's almost like you can look at Barack Obama as the head of a corporation, which is his campaign and if the head of your company is interested in how these technologies can help make better relationships and better business values, it will flow through. This can apply to business people as well, right?

Jascha Franklin-Hodge: Mmhmm, absolutely. One of my favorite examples of this is TiVo, the company that makes the video recorders. Early on, they released a device that was picked up by many early adopters and there was a hacker community online that started to modify these. They started going in these and figured out "Okay, I am going to change this or I am going to put a web server on here" and all that kind of stuff. The traditional response from consumer electronics companies when people open up their boxes is to the lawyers - "shut them down, we can't have that happening."

TiVo took a very different approach, instead of bringing out the lawyers, they said, "That's great, we want you to do this." Not only did they encourage it, but they had some of their engineers and their product people would go and post on these forums. Someone would say, "Hey I hacked my TiVo to do this" and the TiVo folks would say, "Hey, that is a great idea. We are going to look at adding that into the official product." What they were able to do instead of fighting the somewhat chaotic world of the internet and instead embracing it, they were able to build this base of tremendously loyal followers.

In the process, they created a sense of shared responsibility because what the hacker community said was TiVo is being good to us, so we can't use our skills to put them out of business. The one thing that none of the TiVo hackers would do is hack the service so that it was free, because they recognized that if they did that, the partnership that they had established and that good working relationship was not going to function.

I think that it's always a balancing act and this question that you can't just say, "Hey, whatever you want, say whatever you like, do whatever you like." I think that establishing a relationship that respects the community that is built up, whether it is your customers, enthusiasts for your product, by listening to them and engaging them in productive ways. By not feeling that you have to control every aspect of what they do and what they say, they can be able to have a much richer experience. Your customers are more satisfied and you as a business owner can learn a tremendous amount that you would otherwise would have no way to have access to.

Brent Leary: One of the ways that the Obama campaign has reached out and engaged is through www.My.BarackObama.com, the social networking piece of this. Can you talk about how that all worked and how many people are engaging using that particular site?

Jascha Franklin-Hodge: I don't have the total number of unique users off the top of my head, but what we have had is millions of people over the course of this campaign come online and take some kind of action online. An action can vary; some of that is just someone filling out a sign up form saying, "Hey, keep me in the loop." Some of that is people coming in and attending an event, searching through and saying, "Hey, there is a debate watching party in my neighborhood. I want to go and watch the debate with other Obama supporters." Some of those people actually coming online and saying, "I want to organize my neighborhood. I want to be the Boston for Obama guy." So they go and they create a group and they get other people, their friends, their neighbors, other people coming on to the site who are just punching in their zip code to see what is going on around them. They join up and you actually have this whole universe of community organizers, if you will, but leaders within their community who have essentially tapped into this huge base of volunteer effort labor to help organize for the campaign.

We have seen tens of thousands of these groups all around the country. There have been over 150,000 events and most of these have been grassroots events that people just created on their own without the campaign saying, "You, on this day, go do this thing in this place." People said, "Hey, I am going to table at my neighborhood street fair" or "I am going to have a fundraising house party and invite all of my friends to come have dinner and donate to Obama." It's really been tremendously successful in every matrix that we have and I think that the campaign has really said from the onset and throughout this campaign that they really want to embrace that and they want to empower these people. They want to make it possible for them to be the campaign without necessarily having the top-down structure that one would traditionally see.

Brent Leary: Basically, you have created an atmosphere through www.My.BarackObama.com that allowed folks not only to interact with the campaign but to interact with each other and to come up with ideas and implement those ideas, and use www.My.BarackObama.com as the central place for making sure everybody is aware of what is going on.

Jascha Franklin-Hodge: That is exactly it and I think that the strategy that we typically try to employ with all of our clients is one where you recognize that people come in with different levels of engagement. You may have somebody that has been doing political advertising work for twenty years, who knows the ins and outs of their local political world, who comes on and says, "I want to be the local organizer for the campaign." The tools that that person needs, the resources that they need, the encouragement that they need are very different from somebody who just registered to vote last month, who doesn't necessarily know anything about political organizing in practice but who is very excited about the campaign and who wants to play a role in it.

Part of what we try to do is build up the level of engagement and the level of involvement. That means making many different tools available and making sure that peoples' initial contact and then subsequent contacts build from wherever they are and whatever level of engagement that they have. By providing this rich toolset, we are able to engage people who are those first time voters and we are able to engage people that know exactly what they want to do. We are also able to move some of those first-time voters into activists and turn them into real advocates for the campaign.

We have a tool called neighbor-to-neighbor that enables anybody in the country to print out a list of people nearby. It's based on where they live and folks that live near them who are on the list of people that the campaign wants to contact. This is canvassing, a part of political field organizing that's been done since politics existed but what we've done is managed to make it possible at internet scale and we've tried to make it accessible to people that haven't ever done it before. You can go online and you can watch a video that shows you how to do it.

It's easy and just takes a little getting used to, but what we've done is really try to take the whole idea of knocking on your neighbors door and talking about politics and that is something that is accessible to people. Then we have given tools to folks that make it very easy for them to go and print out a list of their neighbors, the questions to ask them. They can go and knock on the doors, they can talk to people, and they can talk to them about why they support Obama. They can find out where they are. All of that data that they have collected gets reported back in an easy to use interface and the campaign then has access to that so that they know that we found an Obama supporter in this neighborhood, but she is going to need a ride to the polls on election day. We can make sure that we get somebody out there with a van, call them up the night before and say, "Hey, what time should we come by?" and give her a ride to the polls.

We are tapping into the power of the internet scale to do this kind of person-to-person interaction. We've tried to do it in a way that people who aren't necessarily professionals or aren't necessarily experienced in this can really step in and say, "I can do this. I want to make a difference. I want to talk to my neighbors. I am going to go for it." That is really been the goal that we've tried to achieve here.

Brent Leary: It's also interesting though you have built this great presence on www.My.BarackObama.com and www.BarackObama.com, how they also embraced going out to where the people are on other networks and using other tools to engage people. For example, the interesting case of how they used text messaging and Twitter originally to announce, "If you want to be among the first to know who our vice presidential candidate is going to be, sign up for a text message or an email." They have integrated a number of the more popular social tools out there. How has that played a role in engagement? I like the other thing that you said too, merging online and offline together.

Jascha Franklin-Hodge: Absolutely, there are many reasons to reach outside of just the website itself. One is simply that not everybody in this country has an internet connection. Now, not everybody has a cell phone, but there are two non-overlapping circles there. There are many people who have cell phones who text all of the time who may access online content via their phone, but don't necessarily have a high speed internet connection in their house. By giving people a way to connect with the campaign via the phones, you open yourself up to a larger audience.

One of the things that you will notice on the text messages that are sent by the campaign, they always say "forward this to a friend." It's trying to tap into the same network effects that we're seeing in the web computer based world, but taking advantage of people's mobile networks. "I text this person all the time. Why don't I just send this one along?" I think that is a piece of what we are trying to do and it's also recognizing that people have different means in which they want to be communicated with.

Certainly when you look among young people there's much greater diversity of tools that they use to interact with their peers, whether it be email, phones, Twitter, instant messenger, social networking sites like Facebook. All of these things are a part of people's lives to varying degrees depending upon who the person is. If we are not there, making the campaign accessible, engaging with people through all of these channels, then we are missing out on a universe of potential supporters of people who may be really enthusiastic about Obama. People who may be really interested in talking to their friends about Obama but just aren't interested in getting emails or aren't interested in one channel or the other and certainly not interested in watching television ads. We are trying to give people that choice to say, "This is how I want to engage; this is how I want to interact with the campaign." As you point out, a piece of this is about merging the online and offline.

One of the things that you will see if you look at the website is the way that these tools are designed. There is not a lot of the functionality that you might see on a site like Facebook, which is great for getting people to talk to each other about their lives but it can be a little bit of a naval-gazing exercise. What we are trying to do with our software is to give people tools that actually discourage them spending all of their time at home talking to people who are already Obama supporters. Instead, doing things within their community that help grow the universe of supporters that in turn helps grow enthusiasm that actually impact votes that impact the campaigns, whether it's talking to your neighbors or if it's fundraising, asking your friends and family to contribute, telling them your story about why you are supporting the campaign. That is all about broadening the community beyond the echo chambers that can spring up in online communities.

The tools are really geared with that idea in mind – its events, its groups, its neighbor-to-neighbor canvassing – it's all these things that really push you outward, not that we want to discourage interaction and organizing online, but that is not the end-all, be-all for any kind of campaign or group that is trying to achieve a specific objective.

Brent Leary: This has been a great conversation with Jascha Franklin-Hodge. Jascha, if you could point out maybe one or two things that as a small business person looking at this - What are a couple of things that they could take away and begin to use for their business to do some of the things that the Obama campaign has done by reaching out and using the web?

Surveys:
Feedback Loops
With Your Market

If you ask the market questions,
you will get answers.

Survey and Polling Tools:

http://www.surveymonkey.com/
http://www.polldaddy.com/
http://buzzdash.com/

Jascha Franklin-Hodge: I think that one of the most important things that we talk to our clients about is creating a feedback loop with people. It's common for businesses to ask their customers what do you think about this or how are we doing, but a lot of times it feels like a one-way conversation. The customer fills out a survey or they fill out a comment card and they don't hear back. They don't see the results of their requests. What we try to do is give people an immediate sense of what it means when they talk to, whether it is a campaign or a non-profit organization, what's that impact like. Some of this is just about conversation, acknowledging that you have heard what they have said and giving them a response, some kind of feedback.

One of my favorite examples of this has really nothing to do with the online world but the bakery around the corner from our office, the woman that runs it takes the comment cards that people put in the box and she writes up responses to them and posts them on the wall. It's a pretty common thing, but the idea there is that you are creating not only a two-way conversation in the sense that yes, somebody is listening to what I am writing, but you are also by sharing that with the larger community of customers. You are allowing people to feel that they are a part of a something. They are not just one person or one voice, but instead they are a part of whole community of people who have opinions, ideas and it becomes a very empowering thing to have that connection and to realize that it's not just you and the business. It's not just you and the candidate, but it's you and everybody else who are all participating in this together.

One example that we've done on the online space, we have a system called grassroots donation matching, which where somebody that may have already given before can say "I'll put up $25 for somebody to match the donation of somebody who has never given." What happens when we do that is you'll get a convenience store clerk in L.A. who gets paired up with a teacher in rural Pennsylvania. It gives people that ability once they've been matched to each other to actually send messages back and forth, talking about "Why I gave" or "Here's what is important to me." The stories that you get out of that, not only in terms of people's individual experiences and their individual reasons for giving but the connections that get made and the commonalities that get found. There is a sense of we may be very different people but we have a lot of the same cares and concerns.

Trying to create those kinds of connections, whether it's between your customers or other people that you are serving with your organization, I think it is really important to tap into this. It doesn't have to be a big fancy social networking system, but even if you ask people for feedback, share some of those responses. If you are doing something in your business because of experiences that you've had or things that your customers have said, tell them about it – tell them why you are doing it. If possible, tell your customers a way to interact with each other. Not only can that sometimes lower your cost from a support or service standpoint, but it helps them understand that they are not alone and there are other people out there that have similar challenges and problems and it helps build the community around your product, service and business.

Brent Leary: Wow that is great information, advice and a great way to have small business people look at the campaign maybe from a different dimension, a dimension that allows them to say, "Hey, you know some of these things, I can do them too." That is really great. Jascha, what would be the one thing that may be the one biggest surprise that you are seeing all of these things taking place and how the technology is being used and the strategies being implemented and everything is being combined, what's been the most surprising outcome from your perspective?

Jascha Franklin-Hodge: That's a good question, I'll confess to a little cynicism here because it's been a tough eight years for Democrats and it's been tough at times to keep the spirits up. What has really surprised me is the extent to which people around the country have, despite the cynicism and frustration that I think a lot of us have felt, managed to come together. It's not in an "Oh God, we have got to get rid of the old guy" but in a real positive light with this campaign and say, "This is somebody that we believe in and somebody that we think is really the right guy. We are excited and we are enthusiastic and we are going to organize and make it happen." Just to watch that progression from somebody who, two years ago, was considered as a real long shot, an outsider, and to watch that community build, that enthusiasm build and to see that succeed... To see that go from a guy with no shot and here we are now a couple weeks out and he is somebody that has got a real shot at the presidency. That, to me, was in some ways less a surprise, but it really lifted some of the cynicism that I've had and gave me faith. Not only in the ability in online community to organize and make something happen and really affect some significant change that people might have said two years ago "that is not possible," the capability of our country as a whole to really embrace that...

I feel no matter what happens on November 4, 2008, I think what we have done here is a tremendous achievement. I also feel a sense of pride and confidence that we are actually going to go forward and we are going to win this thing. To me, if you'd asked me where I would be this time back in February of 2007, this would be what I'd have hoped, but I don't know that I would have said that I expected to be here right now. I think I was really surprised at how much people have come together to make this thing possible.

Brent Leary: Would that have been possible without a strong strategy for embracing the web?

Jascha Franklin-Hodge: I don't think so. Obviously, we have a tremendous candidate and we certainly would not take the full credit by any stretch for the success that Barack has had. I think the core of this campaign and the core of any campaign (but particularly one that doesn't start out with a lot of institutional advantages) is the ability to get people on your side, taking action and to get them organized.

When you are trying to run a national campaign it's really hard to do that without embracing technologies like the internet to get people involved, to get people engaged. Everybody's attention is pulled in so many directions right now, from their family obligations to work to everything else that is going on in their life. You can't just say to people, "If you want to get involved the only way to do it is to spend two Saturdays a month down at our local office." Some people can do that and that's great, but not everybody can do that by tapping into the internet, empowering people in their homes, empowering people in their local communities and giving people these tools. We have really been able to reach and activate a much larger universe of supporters and I think this campaign has really reaped the benefits of that.

Brent Leary: This has been an excellent conversation, Jascha Franklin-Hodge from Blue State Digital. This is powerful information. Jascha let me ask you, where can people learn a little bit more about the background of the story? They can always go to www.BarackObama.com. Is there any other place that they can learn a little bit more about some of the things that we have talked about?

Jascha Franklin-Hodge: To learn about the campaign, go to www.BarackObama.com. If you would like to know more about the technologies and the tools that we are providing, www.BlueStateDigital.com has a lot of information and many case studies, both for political campaigns but also for other types of organizations, including businesses. We definitely are looking to help folks get engaged with their customers, their community and take action.

Brent Leary: Once again, I appreciate your time and the information because the small businesses... I talk to them so much and they are trying to understand the web and how they can use it. They hear a lot about it and stories like this, as you mentioned, somebody who two years ago really wasn't given a chance to get nearly as far as he has. Through what he brings to the table, his strategic vision of how he could leverage the web to get his message out there and get people together, that is a great story for anybody – any small business person. We may be able to do that as well, if somebody else can do it.

Jascha Franklin-Hodge: Absolutely. I think the technology and the potential of this can work at any size organization. The details of how you might implement it are going to be different if you are a 500-customer business or if you are a million customer business. The core ideas of engagement and empowerment are transformative for all kinds of businesses.

Brent Leary: Jascha, thanks again for joining me today.

Jascha Franklin-Hodge: Thank you so much.

You're listening to Technology for Business $ake
Visit www.BusinessTechnologyRadio.com

Podcast Update #10

Xbox Advertising & Tax Calculators

In this podcast, we talk about a few the unique ways Obama's campaign targeted the gaming community by advertising on the billboard of Burnout Paradise - a popular game on the Xbox platform. We also touch on the strategy behind the campaign's Tax Calculator page, as a creative piece of content to reinforce his message to those he's trying to engage. To learn more about these particular moves you may want to check out my blog entry over at Inc.com's Technology Blog - Barack 2.0.

   To read Brent's blog post, please visit:
http://blog.inc.com/technology/2008/10/barack_20.html

Check out this week's podcast as we talk through the lessons you can take from this approach.

   Listen here: http://www.box.net/shared/static/3xc4nv2mes.mp3

   Barack 2.0 Weekly Update #10
Xbox Advertising, Tax Calculators

Brent Leary: Hello and welcome to this week's Barack 2.0 weekly update. I am Brent Leary and with me as always, the man, the myth, the legend, you know him as the online business development expert, David Bullock. How are you doing man?

David Bullock: Brent, I am fine this afternoon, how are you?

Brent Leary: I am doing fine. I am having so much fun just bringing you on. I come up with different things, it's fun. I should have thrown brilliant in there because that word seems to crop up a lot when people talk about you. Anyway, doing fine sir.

David Bullock: {chuckles} Thank you Brent, I appreciate it. On the agenda today, we can see there is a lot going on right now in the world of social media and especially in the way that Barack Obama is moving. We are in the last short strokes – the last thirty days of the election. This is the time when new things are happening. We can bring these to you that you can possibly use with your business. Let's just get right to it. Brent, what do we got?

Brent Leary: Well, we always do the Twitter update to see how many people are following Obama on Twitter. We are closing in on a very interesting milestone, so take it away.

David Bullock: Well, Barack Obama as we speak right now on the 15th of October 2008, at ten minutes to four, Central Standard Time, he is at 98,618 people.

Brent Leary: He is less then fourteen hundred away from 100,000 at this point.

David Bullock: He will be the first person to break 100,000 people following him on Twitter and it will probably happen within the next three or four days, because he is putting on 500 people a day, as far as followers.

Brent Leary: That is incredible, so by the end of this week or the next time we do our show, we should be doing a report that he is over 100,000 followers.

David Bullock: Exactly, right now, Kevin Rose who is at the #2 position is at 67,165. Here is the part that is so interesting to me. He has already done 228 updates.

Brent Leary: That is amazing. He has picked up the pace too on the updates. I have noticed I am seeing more and more frequent updates.

David Bullock: You are right, he is moving around a lot more. It's crunch time and this is the last leg of the campaign.

Brent Leary: Yeah, so next week this time, we will be saying that he has over 100,000 followers.

David Bullock: I am hoping, but we will have that documented and you could say that you heard it here first because we are tracking it on a week-to-week basis.

Brent Leary: He is already following over 100,000.

David Bullock: He is following over 102,000. This again goes back to Twitter etiquette. He is following more people than are following him. People will look into people of who's following them and they will say, "Oh, my Gosh, who is that?" and it's just click, boom. Now they are following him, it's just that easy.

Brent Leary: That is really amazing. Next week we will be giving you the news that he should be over 100,000 followers.

David Bullock: That should be it.

Brent Leary: Let's move on. The campaign is doing many interesting things but before we touch on two of them. Last week, I had the opportunity to talk to Jascha Franklin-Hodge, who is the co-founder and chief technology officer of Blue State Digital. For those who aren't aware or didn't get a chance to listen to that, Blue State Digital is the technology partner of the Obama

Campaign and they are www.BarackObama.com and www.My.BarackObama.com, run off the technology that Blue State Digital provides the campaign. An interesting conversation and I wanted to get your thoughts on what he talked about. It was such an interesting story about how they came together and how the Obama campaign has taken the world by storm on how they are using social media.

David Bullock: I listened to the conversation several times and what I took from it. His story is very much like ours. Eighteen months ago, the Obama fact finders were out there looking around to find out who was going to source this work. Within a week, they found them, boom, site was up and they just started pushing. People think that the campaign started last month or two months ago. This is eighteen months of them doing the work, strategizing, Facebook, MySpace, Twitter and YouTube.

Out of the conversation, what I heard more then anything else was that they had a strategy and they had not wavered from that at all. We are going to create conversation. We are going to allow the people to participate with us. We are going to participate with them. We are going to show up where they are. We are going to help them to engage, become energized and then let them use our platforms to spread our message.

Brent Leary: Yeah.

David Bullock: When I heard it, their strategy was crystal clear from the beginning and then it became tactical implementation of what does that look like? That means we have to be on Facebook. That means we have to be on MySpace. That means we have to use Twitter. That means we have to engage within the blogosphere. Oh and by the way, let us help you to tell your friends about this. Let us help you to go offline with this. The Barack site was set up as a hub for community activism. That is really what it was.

Brent Leary: Absolutely.

David Bullock: They just took the technology that someone would use if they were a community activist trying to do something in their neighborhood and they put it online and then took it to a national audience and said, "If you need help, if you want help, if you want to help, if you need some facilitation, come here."

Brent Leary: That's the key, they made it that not only could they communicate and engage with the folks that were interested in the campaign, they made it to where those folks could communicate and engage in plan and strategize...

David Bullock: ...with each other.

Brent Leary: ...with each other. That's why you are seeing so many different expressions of support and creativity in engaging and telling the story and getting it out, which is just really interesting. It sort of dovetails onto something that just came up that they are doing and it was made really interesting in terms of how people were reacting to it. On Twitter now, they have that site: www.election.twitter.com, people can keep up with the hot keywords that are trending on Twitter. I was looking at the top and I kept seeing Xbox up there.

I kept saying, "What does Xbox have to do with the political climate, the election. What is this?" I clicked and low and behold, the Obama campaign has actual advertising on Xbox, their strategy, their goals, their objectives. They are actually talking to the gamers and they are using their tool of choice, which is the Xbox to do it. David, tell me what you thought about that.

 See Addendum – Figure Web 1.25

 To read the Telegraph related article, please visit:
http://www.telegraph.co.uk/news/newstopics/uselection2008/3198730/Barack-Obama-courts-youth-vote-with-Burnout-Paradise-Xbox-video-game-advertisement.html

David Bullock: When you can go into a game and you see a political advertisement within a game, you are reaching another target market, showing up where your prospects' eyes are. He's in the Xbox version 360 of Burnout Paradise. Big billboard: *Early Voting Has Begun – VoteForChange.com.* He is in a billboard inside of a game.

Brent Leary: {chuckles}

David Bullock: In Indiana where it started, the ad streamed to Xbox gamers. Again streamed, it was coming in real-time from off of the internet platform, coming from the cloud. You have Xbox gamers in Ohio, Florida, Iowa, Colorado, Montana, New Mexico, Nevada and Wisconsin all seeing these ads. Now, look at this. Showing up subliminally – a person in a game having a good time and they see an ad. How susceptible are they to that ad? Very much.

Brent Leary: As I said, it is meeting the people where they are. If you want to engage with certain people, you have to go to where they hang out. You have to talk their language. You have to use their methods of communication and these guys at the Obama campaign have really been effective and creative about doing this. This is just really interesting how they are talking the talk and walking the walk.

David Bullock: The thing that is so interesting, if you look at this and segue this to what normally happens in a movie. We are all familiar with product placement.

Brent Leary: Right

David Bullock: Where you see that soft drink or that advertisement for a particular service, companies pay a lot of money for that product placement in the movies.

Brent Leary: Yeah and it's because it is critical to get to meet the people where they are.

David Bullock: Exactly.

Brent Leary: That's one aspect. Here is another thing that they are doing. The focus is on the economy. Everybody focuses on their plans and what does it mean in terms of are we going to have credit, so we can borrow to buy cars and houses. Are we going to have job growth so we will feel comfortable about having jobs? The economy is so critical. One of the things that they just recently did is they put this on their website.

David Bullock: The calculator

 To view the Obama Tax calculator, please visit http://taxcut.barackobama.com/

Brent Leary: Yeah, the economic calculator that talks about and answers some of their critics that say that they are just going to increase your taxes. They use this page on their site to say hey, first 95% of the people are going to get tax breaks or something like that. Then they have a calculator to give you an idea of what to expect. That is really interesting.

 See Addendum – Figure Web 1.26

David Bullock: It's another form of user generated content and a calculator. When you are talking about people's money, a calculator is the ultimate engagement device.

Brent Leary: Yes

David Bullock: One of the other things that I noticed when I was looking at the site calculator is they also have a link from the Obama site out to the opponent's site. This is saying - here is his explanation of the very same thing that we are showing you a calculation on.

 See Addendum – Figure Web 1.27

Instead of pushing away from the competition, they have a link to the competition, so that the person can make an educated decision about what they are going to do.

Brent Leary: That's key because what they are saying is, "Look, we have nothing to hide, we want you to be informed, we want you to know what is going on with the other side. We want you to take a look and see how it compares." That shows us a level of confidence that hey, we think we have a better handle on this and we want you to get an understanding of that. You need to check out what the other guy is doing and then you can see that we know what we are doing.

David Bullock: There is something else going on here. If you look at some of the basic tenets of web 2.0 nomenclatures, just a foundational culture, you are talking about authenticity and transparency. You will hear those words batted around. What that means is you need to be true to what you say and what you do, but you are also going to let people see you doing what you say and what you do. You are going to open up the book and say, what I know is what you know.

It's about sharing information.   There is a blatant mistrust of large corporations, politics and people in general. When you start opening up your doors to see what you're thinking, doing and let them find out for themselves – you allow them a level of confidence, not only in them but in you, because you are now the tour guide to a decision you want to help them make.

Brent Leary: Absolutely, so once again we just rattled off about two or three really great lessons that every small business can take something away from. It's really important. We cannot stress this enough to look at what is going on, not just solely from a political perspective, that's important too, but if you are a business person, take a different look – use a different dimension here. All of these things you can put in play for your small business.

David Bullock: Understand something and I want to stress this. This is a business development -business lesson that we are extracting from the marketplace what we see that is effectively being utilized from this campaign for you to make the distinctions to use them for your business. Who wins is going to be who wins. At the end of the day, your business has to prosper through whatever happens, the bailout, the economic forecast, whatever happens on Wall Street. Your business has to move well with the new technologies. That is what we are trying to bring forth for you.

Brent Leary: This has been another weekly update on Barack 2.0. I hope you guys are enjoying this. I hope you are seeing some benefit from it. I think David and I are definitely seeing some benefit from it. We are sort of living the dream here folks. Everything we are seeing we are trying to put into play ourselves. I hope you are doing it too. We love to hear from you, please leave us some feedback, some comments on the site at www.Barack20.com. Once again, if there is something that you would like for us to cover or take a look at, let us know. We would love to do it.   David, any parting words as we end this week.

David Bullock: We are getting close to the end, we are going to continue as things heat up we will continue to do these reports. Let's pay attention, there is a lot of good information here and we are really having a good time bringing it to you. Thank you so much.

Brent Leary: See you next week for another Barack 2.0 weekly update, thanks again.

Podcast Update #11

Final Words Before The Big Day

This podcast is the last one before the election. David and I cover a lot of ground here, as well as take a look back at the last three months of doing these weekly updates. We discuss the impact of Michelle Obama's blogging on BlogHer.org. How the campaign is still marrying offline/online activities. In addition, David and Brent each share their personal observations as to what was the most important lesson to take away from analyzing Obama's campaign - a campaign that led Ad Age to name Obama as their marketer of the year.

To read Ad Age's Article, please visit:
http://adage.com/moy2008/article?article_id=131810

It was also one of the driving factors in Brent writing a white-paper you may want to read, entitled Social CRM - Customer Relationship Management in the Age of the Socially-Empowered Customer.

To read Brent's whitepaper, please visit:
http://www.box.net/shared/static/adqb9k3pqy.pdf

David and I are also pleased to let you know that the Barack 2.0 site was featured in the November issue of Black Enterprise as part of an article discussing the Obama campaign's use of technology. Thank you all for your great interest and support. David and I are extremely appreciative too for your kind words and comments.

"Weekly listener and full time follower of both Brent and David on Twitter.
Barack Obama's social media team has done it again.
These lessons are very inspiring.
I plan on using many if not all to help broaden my social media experience."

Jeff Brathwaite - www.2thenextlevel.com

Check out this week's podcast as we talk through the lessons you can take from this approach.

Listen here: http://www.box.net/shared/static/3uxpopnh6x.mp3

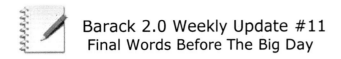

Barack 2.0 Weekly Update #11
Final Words Before The Big Day

Brent Leary: Hello and welcome to the latest installment of the Barack 2.0 weekly update. I am Brent Leary and as always, along with me today and it's sort of chilly out there too, I don't know if it's chilly in Tennessee, but it is cold here. We have the Internet-Marketing Guru. I am quoting from Black Enterprise right now, the internet-marketing guru, Mr. David Bullock. How are you doing sir?

 See Addendum – Figure Web 1.28

David Bullock: Good morning Brent, I am fine on this chilly day in October. I believe this is the last full week before – many things are happening in the marketplace that we can report on.

Brent Leary: Absolutely, but before we get to all of that. Let's get the Twitter Weekly Update of how many people are following Mr. Barack Obama.

David Bullock: Twitter update for today, he has 108,979 people following him on Twitter with 248 updates. A very peculiar thing has happened. We were using a tool called www.Twitterholic.com that was checking to see who the most followed person on Twitter was. That listing that had Barack Obama at the top was upwards of 40,000 above the next person. That listing has been removed since last week.

Brent Leary: That is interesting; we have got to find out what the deal is behind that. It's fascinating how he got – did anybody else at the top get removed?

David Bullock: No, everybody is still there like Leo Leporte and those guys, they are still in the same spot. In fact, let me check right now while I am thinking about it.

Brent Leary: It seemed like Kevin Rose was in second place.

David Bullock: Ah, this morning he is back, but he was gone.

Brent Leary: I hope there are no dirty campaign tricks going on here.

David Bullock: I don't know, but for a couple of days he was not listed at the very top, but he is back at the top, doesn't matter. The next person in line is at 69,750.

Brent Leary: Wow, so he is almost 40,000 up on the next person.

David Bullock: That's pretty impressive.

Brent Leary: Absolutely, because when we first started looking at this, he was in second or third place and when we started looking at this, he may have had 50,000 followers.

David Bullock: Exactly

Brent Leary: He is over that in about a two month time period, he picked up 57,000 followers.

David Bullock: The first person to hit the 100,000 person mark on Twitter. Here is the other thing that has become very interesting. Twitter has become now very much – I don't want to say a household word, but in CNN and some of the major news outlets. They are using Twitter to get feedback from the marketplace.

Brent Leary: Yeah, absolutely. I wrote for the American Express open forum blog, this was when Hurricane Gustav was about to hit and how Rick Sanchez over at CNN was incorporating the Twitter community into his broadcast. We are seeing even more and more and that's just the way it is going to be from now on.

David Bullock: Twitter is out there.

Brent Leary: Let's jump into it, we are in the last week as you mentioned and it's been fascinating looking at how the Obama campaign is using all the tools in their chamber so to speak to really get their message. He is calling it his closing argument, I think is the term he is using.

David Bullock: Oh yeah.

Brent Leary: He is using that term, but he is using all the tools to get that term across.

David Bullock: Absolutely, what is happening now is every media channel, if you really take a step back and look at what is happening here. Every media channel right now is being used for promotion - magazines, bumper stickers, infomercials – which is coming tonight. You have so much going out. The entire web is being used, all social media. As a business owner, how can you get your message out on all channels as inexpensively as possible so you are present? My little girl was in the bookstore, we were looking at the magazine rack, and she made a statement that really took me aback. She said, 'Barack Obama is everywhere."

Brent Leary: {chuckles}

David Bullock: That speaks to him being ubiquitous, he is everywhere. His promotional channels have completely saturated the minds of the community. He is out here.

Brent Leary: Absolutely and like you said, it's in every facet. You mentioned the infomercial that is going to be on six or seven major networks tonight. There is also, I'll plug us a little bit, because we were recently featured in the latest Black Enterprise issue that is really focused on Barack Obama, but they had a special piece on how he is using technology and they gave us a little plug there. One of the things, as I was going into the bookstore over the weekend to find the magazine, I was struck by how many covers had him on the front. It was just amazing. It was like in the Barnes and Noble in the Atlanta metro area, there was a special stand and there were maybe nine or ten magazines on there. He was on eight of the covers.

David Bullock: Amazing

Brent Leary: It's amazing, he is on TV. He is on magazines. As we like to talk about, he is on the web. I noticed one thing about his tweets, he has actually picked up the pace with the tweets that have been coming out. So he is not just relying solely on the major outlets, he has always been in tune with the web and he hasn't stopped that a bit. In fact, we were just talking, one of the interesting things, it's not just him. It's Michelle Obama.

David Bullock: Right and she showed up and I know we are going to talk about what she is doing now. She showed up on Larry King and I was able to sit and watch the amount of activity that was created from her showing up on the late night television shows. Look at the situation here, not only is he promoting, she's promoting on and in the major channels for media distribution.

Brent Leary: Not only that, but she's also creating and giving her side of the story and using the web to do that. Just yesterday, once again, www.election.Twitter.com allows you to see what is going on right as it is taking place. I have that up and I noticed her name was trending as one of the key trends – keywords in Twitter. I clicked on it and there is a list of people talking about, you've got to see the blog entry that Michelle Obama put out on www.BlogHer.com.

David Bullock: Wow

Brent Leary: Now www.BlogHer.com is one of the, maybe the top site for women bloggers. I think she has done two or three posts. She just did one this week and it really caught the attention of the BlogHer community. That is once again, those are some intellectual outstanding women bloggers. Not only the bloggers, but the people who read it are really in tune and engaged. For her to spend some time talking and sharing their story with that audience, once again, that is that target focus, that laser focus of talking to people on their turf, using their tools, using their language, to get your message across and to engage them. So yeah, they are on TV, they are on radio, but they are still using the web as it has never been used before. We have never seen this type of interaction.

 To read Michelle Obama's blog posts, please visit:
http://www.blogher.com/one-week-change

David Bullock: No, the involvement is incredible and one of the things that I really wanted to notice that she has wrapped her message in a way that it can be consumed by the community that she is speaking to.

Brent Leary: Yes

David Bullock: How many times do we have a message that we massage it the way we want it to be put out, as opposed to the way it can be heard, it can be listened, will be consumed, but more importantly, will be accepted because you are almost doing it right in the person's living room. Think about that for a minute.

Brent Leary: Absolutely

David Bullock: When you show up at someone's house, there is an etiquette that you have to maintain while you are in their situation. They are going right into people's situations and speaking to them the way they want to be spoken to. That analogy for marketing along the lines of segmentation, tailoring your message to exactly what needs to be heard, wants to be heard, and will be accepted by the listener. I mean, if you look at it that way, look at the website and see how it is segmented. Look at how he is moving in the marketplace. Notice he is not on one major channel. He is on all of them because everyone is not looking at only one in particular. They may be tuned in over here, so he is going to show up where they are. Notice that he is showing up where the people are with his message. She is showing up where people are with not only the message, but the message wrapped up in the special way that she can deliver it to that audience. That is the lesson there.

Brent Leary: I will add just one more thing on top of that. It's also, people like it when you show them the attention. You come into their neighborhood and you go to them. In terms of the infomercial tonight, yeah, he is going on MSNBC, CBS and Fox and all that, but he also bought time on BET and he also bought time on Telemundo. He isn't sticking to the big networks. He is going to the targeted networks because that shows some respect to those folks.

David Bullock: Exactly

Brent Leary: Just like her blogging on BlogHer, that shows respect because she thinks enough about that community of women bloggers and influential women that she's going not only to talk to them, but she is going to where they are to talk to them.

David Bullock: She is going to the house.

Brent Leary: For small business people, those are some excellent lessons that we can use. We aren't ever going to be on a scale of what these folks are doing, but we don't need to be. There are plenty of opportunities and outlets for us to be able to effectively communicate our message to the people we are trying to reach.

David Bullock: Notice something else, he is not just using online, but they are still on the phone calling and still using direct mail. Notice this; this is the last day for solicitation that they can solicit in the marketplace for donations. They did $150 million last month and that was all with the average person giving $100. That is a lot of promotion and many donations.   He is still pressing the market, even up to the last day. He has not let up on his marketing.

Brent Leary: Yes

David Bullock: He has not attained the goal. If you are a business owner, until you have obtained the goal, until the phone is ringing at the level you want it to ring. Until the sales are coming the way you want them to come, you have to keep pressing against the mark. If you look at the polls, the way that it is set up right now, technically, he is ahead, he is winning, technically, but he is not letting go.

As a business owner, lot of times we get into a situation where it is working and it's almost complacency with our marketing. No, no, no. Marketing is an effort. I was at a place called BarCamp – Nashville within the last two weekends I presented some of the lessons we are highlighting here on these calls to the audience there – a group of business owners on the tech side. A question came up, well we don't have $300 million, we are not a U.S. Senator, we can't do what he has done. I simply responded saying, "you can do what he has done – maybe not at the same scale, but he didn't start at $300 million. He didn't start as a senator. He started where he was with the idea, decided on a message, and decided to push it into the marketplace."

Every business owner can take that lesson and say, no matter where you are now, whether you are prominent in the marketplace, you don't have a big budget, it doesn't matter. You can get started now and actually make a difference and push your message and your model forward.

Brent Leary: So when that guy came to you like that, you know what you should have said?

David Bullock: What

Brent Leary: Just three words – Yes, We Can

David Bullock: Yes, We Can.

{chuckles}

David Bullock: Well, I could have that would have been the one-liner that would have ended all things. In that moment, one of the things that happened is, it made me go back and do some more research.

Brent Leary: Yeah

David Bullock: Notice as you are confronted with a situation and you really don't know the answer, one thing that you can do on the web is you can find out. Now, here it is this morning I am taking my little girl to school. What did I notice? I am seeing signs in people's yards, bumper stickers and buttons. Again, not that the business owner can do all of that but you can get paraphernalia. People can wear your ball caps or your t-shirts. They will put a bumper sticker on. You can do some of these things, just scale it back, and look at what is going on because this is probably the most successful marketing initiative ever.

Brent Leary: Well, we'll hold judgment until next week, but it's been wildly successful as it is. I think next week will let us know if it's actually *the* most successful.

David Bullock: Okay, that's a bit of hyperbole – *the most*. I will put it this way, for using technology, using social media, this is up to date a very well executed plan, strategic initiative and it's been executed, I won't say flawlessly because you don't really know what is going on out there behind the scenes, but it is working. It seems to be doing something in the marketplace. It is moving the needle.

Brent Leary: This is going to be our last update before the election. David, let me ask you and I'll tack onto it afterwards. What have you learned the most? What has been the most important lesson over these last several months of watching this? What has been the thing that really stood out to you?

David Bullock: I must first say that I have learned more in the last several months that we have been tracking this because as you know, I am in the back going deeper into the technology of what is really going on and what is the infrastructure. I've learned that you really can create a situation that becomes a machine that just works on all channels. You can engage your public and they will engage with you if you show up the right way, where they are.

I have also discovered that there is more then just one channel. There is a multitude of channels if we decide to go look for them and on those channels may be is one new customer. If you are on fifty channels, you may pick up fifty customers. A case in point, I just did some work based on some of the things that we have been studying here. I did some work with a local company and was able to produce 100 new leads in a 48 hour period – just by tapping into a channel they already had access to but weren't using. I am becoming keenly aware of all of these channels. We have outlined at least 120 channels so far and there are probably more. At least these are the ones that we can see and put a name on.

Brent Leary: Absolutely

David Bullock: That is what I have learned. You can get your message out and the key is not to have one way to get a hundred people, necessarily, but to have a hundred ways to get one person and connect effectively with that one person. At the end of the day, that one person multiplied is your customer base.

Brent Leary: Yeah, that is awesome. I think what I take away from all of the different great lessons. I mean it is almost hard to pick one. One of the things that I take away that I wasn't really sure of, but I definitely am now – we as small business people, we can do whatever we need to and want to in order to get our message out – get our idea out. We are a perfect example of that actually. What started as an article, an online article around we were fascinated with what was going on and how the Obama campaign has been using it. It started out as an article and turned into a powerpoint presentation, a webinar, a website, a podcast series, a couple of hundred dollars of commitment and investment and maybe an hour or two a week of time investment has turned into something that has put us into places that I don't think we were really expecting to go.

David Bullock: Yes

Brent Leary: We are two guys that had an idea that used regular means of communication, morphed that into the web, took that idea to the web and let other people judge whether it was something of interest and let them find it on their own. They found it. They liked it. Because of that, we are not just able to just report about it, we are actually living it. I think that is the thing that I took away from it the most. We were actually able to look at what he did and use some of the tools and strategies that the campaign has used and we are walking, living testaments that this stuff can work for the little guy. That is what I really took away from it.

David Bullock: You make a fascinating point there. It did start with an idea. It started with us saying, "Hey, let's see" It was something that we were interested in and that you are interested in as a business owner. You are interested in your business and it can become so much more if you package the right way and you are getting in front of the right people and you are doing it with some type of a system.   Every week or week and a half we are doing this, it's consistent, it keeps moving. We did it right, we utilized technology. Brent you are saying it right, it started from an idea to a national magazine spot and it occurred in less than ninety days, because that's when this site went up, July 30, 2008 was the site launch date.

Brent Leary: In August, yep, absolutely. We are living testaments that this can happen. The story isn't over yet folks, believe me, it may just be getting started if we put it like that. I think if you could take away some of the things that we talked about just now but go back and listen to some of the podcasts that we had. Maybe check out some of the writings. You may see that

Hey, this stuff can actually work for you. It worked for us. We are no different. We are small business people just like you guys are and we had an idea.

I think we were able to piggyback on the national attention that the Obama campaign was drawing, but we looked at it from a different angle and our perspective of this is great and interesting but maybe this is something we do need to start taking advantage of ourselves as business people. We were able to piggyback off the national attention but we were always focused on what we do best. I think if you do that, if you can somehow tie in something that is drawing a lot of attention, maybe you find out how it fits what you really do and then start to put it out there and begin to study it. Start to strategize around that. Maybe it will work for you as well as it seems to be working for us.

David Bullock: Let me just interject there. In every industry, in every business sector, there is a prominent story. There is something in that particular sector or industry that people really do care about on a human level, on an emotional level. The key is for you to take the time to find out what that story is. Once you take that story and you wrap it up again in a way that people can get it, understand it and are willing to consume it. That is your opening into the conversations that you want to have. You can start over here and end up over there once you are in the conversation.

As I am listening, I am going back and seeing that you can use these materials to start the conversation with the prospects and clients that you want to engage with. Marketing opens up the door for conversation, the technology and the media are the carrier of that message that opens the conversation. Use the stuff and start the conversation and then once you are in there you can take them anywhere you want to. You can find out what they are interested in. You can move them to closure. You can refer them to services, but again, you have to start with the conversation and that starts with you being interested and interesting to them.

Brent Leary: Absolutely, so folks this is the last one before the big day. Afterwards, we will do one last one, like a post mortem of what happened and what may happen in the future. This has been your Barack 2.0 Weekly Update folks. As always, we love to hear from you. We would like to thank you first for all of the comments that we have been receiving and we would love to see more, so please continue to send us your feedback and stay tuned to next week's final edition of the Barack 2.0 Weekly Update. Thanks again.

Commentary

Successful Social CRM and Superior Marketing in Practice

The first presidential campaign to fully embrace the ideas and practices of social media has met with a successful end. Senator Barack Obama has been elected the 44th President of the United States of America.

This punctuates the successful use of social media for the promotion of a message into the marketplace. Communication has evolved.

It is not days to get a message via pony express. Now it is in an instant.

This is what social media is all about. This campaign is the product of superior multi-channel audio, video and text content distribution using **new and traditional media** platforms.

- **Get** the message out.

- **Keep** the message fresh.

- **Stick** to the story.

- **Track** and stay in touch with the interested visitor.

- **Develop** a worthwhile engaging relationship with those who can support you and your concerns.

These are just a few of the (many) lessons illustrated with this successful campaign. To all those that have taken the time to visit and comment as we moved with this case study - Thank You. We have learned much from this experience.

David Bullock

Director of Online Research
www.Barack20.com

Brent Leary and David Bullock

Conclusion

Analyzing the Most Successful Internet Marketing Campaign Ever

The reports for the campaign are being published and there will be much "Monday Morning Quarterbacking" on how these online fund raising results were achieved.

As Brent Leary and David have been following this story from the very beginning, we have seen how these numbers grew week by week.

Per the story run by the Washington Post, this is a brief summary of the Obama Campaign online operations stats:

- 3 million online donors
- 6.5 million online donations adding up to more than $500 million
- Of the 6.5 million donations, 6 million were in amounts of $100 or less
- Upwards of 13 million addresses were captured
- More than 1 billion e-mails sent during the campaign
- Approximately 1 million mobile phone numbers collected
- 2 million profiles created on the www.My.BarackObama.com social network
- 5 million supporters on other social networking and multimedia sharing sites

These are the fantastic results of the campaign. No doubt this will be a topic of conversation for years to come.

The question is...

Now that you have seen power of traditional, social and internet marketing, what actions will you take to learn and use these available tools and concepts to successfully promote your business?

There are many lessons here hidden within this ultra successful campaign, if you have the distinctions to see them. Personally, I have learned more about marketing within the last 18 months than I have in the last 10 years. Experiencing the power of a well executed multi-channel campaign can change the way that you approach the promotion of your business.

Check out this week's podcast as we talk through the lessons you can take from this approach.

 Listen here: http://www.box.net/shared/static/orcps7o2lq.mp3

 The Most Successful Internet
Marketing Campaign Ever

Brent Leary: Hello and welcome to what is going to be the final, I can't believe it, I am already starting to tear up, the final weekly update for the Barack 2.0 website. I am Brent Leary and as always, he is here, all the way from Tennessee, the online marketing business development guru extraordinaire, the brilliance is just radiating right here, I can see it all the way from Atlanta. It is David Bullock. How are you doing, Sir?

David Bullock: Doing well today.

Brent Leary: We took a couple of weeks off because we just wanted to soak in everything after the election and sort of analyze stuff is what we like to do. Can you believe that we are at the last Barack 2.0 Weekly Update?

David Bullock: Well, it's a wonderful thing that we can get to the last one and we actually can punctuate it with a win.

Brent Leary: We can now say, because I was a little hesitant, you weren't, that this would be known as the most successful internet marketing campaign ever. I think that we can actually say that it is.

David Bullock: Oh, it is. Right now what is so interesting is the pundants are now looking back almost like a Monday morning quarterback situation to say, well, here is what happened. You had to get what was happening as it was happening, so that now you can really know what happened. We were looking at it day-to-day, we have over 500 documents here, showing what was going on in the space both online and offline from the very beginning. For all of those getting last numbers, the numbers are the results of what actually occurred and we were actually from day one. We have used it on our site to push it out into the marketplace.

Brent Leary: Yeah, we are going to get into some of those numbers too, but before we do that. There was a number that we had been tracking all throughout every podcast we did. It was how many people were following him on Twitter. Why don't we do just one last count for that.

David Bullock: The Twitter update for today the 23rd of November, 2008, we are looking at Barack Obama the people who are following him are 140,000 that he is following. His followers are now at 136,193. Again, he is following 140,000 and 136,000 are following him. The etiquette of him being interested in what people are saying and doing and whom he is following, still reigns. He is still doing the very same things now as he was doing before the account even took off.

Brent Leary: All right

David Bullock: He is following more people than are following him.

Brent Leary: I think we started doing this back in early August, when we did the very first podcast and if I can recall, he was in that 45,000 to 50,000. So we are talking about him gaining over 100,000 people over the course of those three months that we've been looking at this.

David Bullock: Imagine that. You have to look at the fact that he's gotten such a following because he was using several modes of communication into the marketplace. He wasn't just using Twitter. He wasn't just using social networks. He was using the radio and television. Any time you would find him, it all pointed back to Twitter or any of the things that he was using. The blogosphere, as you know, was a buzz with the fact that he was following people. That was a story in and of it self, which lends itself to the lesson of creating news out of news and making that news viral.

Brent Leary: Let's talk a little bit about some of the numbers now that the campaign is officially over and he's won, you found some really interesting statistics. Give us a few of the baseline numbers that he was able to accomplish.

David Bullock: These numbers are coming from a story that was run by the Washington Post just this week, but as you know, we actually interviewed the guys over at Blue State Digital, so we saw these numbers growing.

 To read the Washington Post Article, please visit: http://voices.washingtonpost.com/the-trail/2008/11/20/obama_raised_half_a_billion_on.html

He had 3,000,000 people that donated online. 6.5 million online donations adding up to more then a half a billion dollars, that's 500 million dollars.

Brent Leary: Say that again.

David Bullock: 6.5 million donations adding up to more then 500 million dollars collected.

Brent Leary: Wow

David Bullock: That is just online. That does not count the people who signed up online and then got a telephone call. Or signed up online and got a direct mail piece. Or signed up online and got a text message. Do you see what I am saying?

Brent Leary: Yeah

David Bullock: Those numbers are huge, but that is just the online side.

Brent Leary: Yep

David Bullock: Of those 6.5 million donations, 6 million of them were in amounts of $100 or less. That means that this was a full team effort. This is volume selling, when you are getting a lot of people doing a little bit.

Brent Leary: Yeah, even Joe the Plumber could have afforded that, right?

David Bullock: Exactly. He had upwards of 3 million email addresses that he captured. This goes to the fact that he now has a mailing list online, which is an extraordinary amount of people who are interested in what he was trying to do and probably still interested now.

Brent Leary: Yeah, I don't think it stops with him winning.

David Bullock: No, he has left the site up.

Brent Leary: Yeah

David Bullock: The site is still there, so it is still working for him. More than 1 billion emails were sent during the campaign that is 1 billion with a "b." Approximately 1 million mobile phone numbers were collected. That's another mailing list, another way to communicate directly with the people, right in their pocket. 2 million profiles were created on www.My.BarackObama.com. He created a social network within a social network and then outside of his social network, 55 million supporters on other social networking and multimedia sites. Look at this, millions upon millions and that is just on the online side. Let's look at this, people communicate with people, the conversation started online and ultimately it moved to an offline result and that is the real lesson here. Yes, a lot of things happened online but it all moved ultimately to an offline result in the marketplace.

Brent Leary: Yeah, I think also it is really critical to point out to folks that these numbers are fantastic, but don't get discouraged because nobody else will ever be able to do what he did again.

David Bullock: Exactly, this was a perfect storm, this was a nexus. Look at this; you had an economy that was doing something. You had the field that pared its way down. You had a situation before him with the current presidency that people were disgruntled with. You had the African American turnout. You had people who had never voted before. You had young people energized. You had user generated content. You had all of this stuff, so will this ever happen again this way? No, but like you said Brent, and you are absolutely correct.

At scale, any business can utilize the very same tools, techniques, strategies and tactics that he used. What he used in the marketplace was good solid communication. He kept to his message. He kept true to his brand. He keep repeating the same message over and over and over again and more important than anything else, he used any means possible to do one thing and one thing only, start the conversation and be connected with the people he was in communication with.

Brent Leary: Yeah, it is critically important for folks to understand those numbers just tell you how well it worked for him. It's important, just from that standpoint to know it worked. I would not even concentrate on the numbers, once you understand that it worked for him on the scale that it worked for, that is all you really need to know. The second part that you need to know is why it worked for him and David you just hit on it. He had a clear concise message that he shared with people through every means imaginable. He didn't just share it with people, he invited them in to be a part and to help him to shape the message and communicate the message to the folks they know. Those are the biggest takeaways that you can find.

    a.) These technologies can work
    b.) You have to have the right message and the right motive for those technologies to work for you.

Don't get caught up in the scale, but get caught up in the fact that you can use this and you can engage people and if you are really truly open to bi… I don't want to say bipartisan because then we are getting back into the politics. But if you are open to open communication…

David Bullock: Dialogue

Brent Leary: Yeah dialogue, not monologue, dialogue to really listen to people as well as talk to them and engage them and allow them to work with your message and to shape your message as much as you want it to be shaped, but be open to the flexibility. It allows you to create relationships that go way beyond a vendor/customer type of thing, but this goes to advocacy, to partnerships and realty meaningful relationships.

David Bullock: One of the things that I would like to say is I have learned more in the last several months, analyzing and looking at this campaign that I have learned in both offline and online sales. Because if you looked at the end, there was an emotional impact that this campaign had on people. You could see them in tears. You could see them joyous, happy and sad. You saw all the range of emotions based on just a message, a possibility of being promoted into the marketplace. Your business message, your unique selling proposition, what you do in the marketplace. The question that you have to ask yourself is do you have a story that touches people and can it make a difference in peoples' lives and can you stand behind that story and promote it honestly and ethically into the marketplace.

Forget about the politics and just take that lesson and look at your business. If you have something worth talking about, use the technologies that are available now to get that conversation in the marketplace, because people know you by your content. They will trust you by your content and they will act with you based on how you are positioned within the marketplace.

The very first conversation that Brent and I did, when we talked about your Google Quotient, how are you known online. Having that reputation online is really what this thing boils down to. Once you put it out there, people start to know you by your content. They may not know you, but they know what you are putting out there by your podcasts, your videos, your blog posts, by your articles. All of that stuff out there speaks for you before you show up and that's the mechanism that you see at play here.

Brent Leary: Yeah, these are the basic principles of social CRM folks:

    a.) People like doing business with people they like

It can't get any straighter than that: How much easier it is for you to pull out your wallet and give your money over to somebody that you like.

b.) People love doing business with people they trust.

It makes it so much easier, you can sleep better at night, if you know that the folks you are in business with, that you depend on to supply you and help you get your customers and your revenue stream, If you can depend on them when you need them. If you can get people to like you and trust you, you have got a great case for bringing them on as a customer. Now what Barack and his team were able to do was use technology to reach millions of people with their message and invite them in under the tent. We have to figure out how we can use technology to do just those same things because we need to get people to like us and trust us, so content can open that door to a conversation. That conversation can build into meaningful exchanges and those exchanges can convert that stranger into a customer. We can only do that, like David says, if we can provide content that will be engaging, captivating and that will make people reach out to us. Just like Barack and his team were able to put content together that brought folks to their side to listen, communicate and exchange and then to go out and be the feet on the street and knock on doors and create events. All of those kinds of things we can do on a much smaller scale of course, but we can do that too. That is what the golden message – the biggest take away we could ask for you to really look into when it comes to this stuff.

David Bullock: Yeah, this has been a fascinating study. We have shown you in action: Facebook, YouTube, Blip.tv, UStream, Twitter, FriendFeed, Meetup, Flickr, MySpace and LinkedIn. This has been a case study on exactly what was happening as it was happening. Yes, we brushed over the surface and these have been summaries.

There is so much more information and so many more lessons that we have extracted and documented, but if you just take these takeaways and move forward with your business, you don't need a million people calling in orders for your business to be successful. You may only need a couple hundred or a couple thousand, but the technology is here. You now have a mini-blueprint of the blueprint. Yes, there is a lot to know. There is a lot of how to's here.

We have shown you what he did and the results, but there is a lot to know about how to do it. There is etiquette to know here. There are techniques to know here. There is SEO, Search Engine Optimization, copyrighting, CRM and salesmanship. There are a lot of underlying things to know to make this really work. We implore you and invite you to look over the site, give us comments.

We won't be doing any more of these posts, this way going over what he's done because he has done it; it's over at this point. We will be checking back in because now there is a next part of the story that we are pushing on now because we have used the techniques that we have learned to promote this site and a very exciting adventure has opened up on our side and we will be letting you know about it as we move forward.

Brent Leary: Absolutely, folks these lessons aren't necessarily over because Barack is still using technology. One of the things that we know is that you need to check out www.change.gov. He opened that the day after the election was over. That is one of those places you can learn more about what he is doing. We have also learned not too far back, within the last couple of days, I believe he just did his first one is that he is going to be doing his weekly radio address but they are also going to be on YouTube.

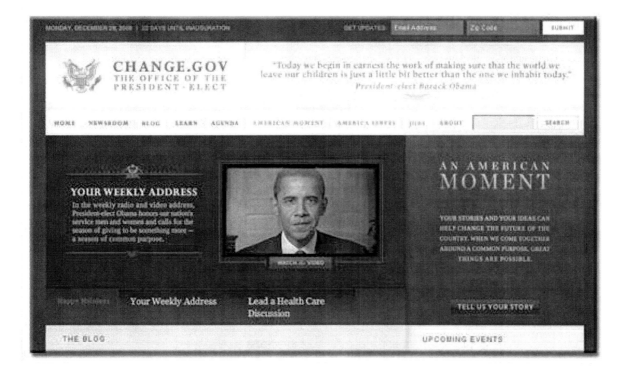

David Bullock: Mmhmm

Brent Leary: Once again, he won, but he knows it's not over. This is like how can you stop using the telephone just because you used it back in the fifties for the first time. You continue to use it because it is a way to communicate. Keep that in mind and also as David said. This is not necessarily the last you are going to hear from us. Stay tuned, we are actually going to be asking you to help us out on one of our initiatives, so please stay tuned for that. David, any last parting words for the last Barack 2.0 Weekly Update?

David Bullock: Thank you so much for your time and attention over this case study that we have been doing for the last several months it has been more then a pleasure to bring this information to you. It's been fun Brent, putting this on. I am glad we had an idea and I am glad that we took action. Folks, we invite you to do the same thing. Get the idea, develop the story, use any means possible to get it out and take action. That is the key.

Brent Leary: It was great running into you in May, back at the Black Enterprise Entrepreneurs conference. I am glad that we were also looking at this whole Barack thing and we were inspired to keep our eyes open for it and I am definitely glad for the last four months of going through this. It's been a pleasure. I have learned as much in that four or five month period then I can imagine in any five or ten year period. I look forward to learning more as we go along. This has been the last Barack 2.0 weekly update, thank you for all of your comments and thank you for listening.

Final thought from Brent Leary:

It is now official - President-elect Barack Obama has authored the most successful Internet marketing campaign ever. He and his campaign have gone from the longest of long-shots, to the presidency in less than two years. His campaign's embrace of technology has played a key role in spreading his message of hope and change to millions of people - people looking to be a part of that change.

David Bullock and I have had the pleasure of watching this unfold and sharing some of things that piqued our curiosity with respect to just how Obama and his team utilized a dizzying array of tools and strategies. We've learned a great deal in studying the campaign, and we hope you learned along with us. In fact, we know you did, based on the many comments you've shared with us.

We are greatly appreciative of all of you who've visited the site. We've been consistently surprised by all the interest people have shown in the business lessons coming out of this historical campaign. We're glad to have learned with you and from you.

Although this is the last Barack 2.0 Update, this is not the last you will hear from us, as we have some exciting things we'll be announcing in the near future - so please stay tuned!

Thanks again for all of your support. David and I appreciate you all.

About the Authors

Brent Leary and David Bullock are the creators of Barack 2.0 (www.Barack20.com), a website dedicated to analyzing the Obama campaign's use of social media from a small business perspective. The two were recently featured in Black Enterprise magazine for their coverage of Obama's technology moves.

Meet Brent Leary

Brent Leary is a customer relationship management industry analyst, advisor, speaker and award winning blogger. He is co-founder and Partner of CRM Essentials LLC, an Atlanta based CRM advisory firm covering tools and strategies for improving business relationships.

Recognized by InsideCRM as one of 2007's 25 most influential industry leaders, Leary also received CRM Magazine's Most Influential Leader Award in 2004. He serves on the national board of the CRM Association, and as a subject matter expert for the Small Business Technology Task Force.

He's been quoted in several national business publications, including the Wall Street Journal, Newsweek and Entrepreneur magazine.

Leary writes regular online columns for Inc. and Black Enterprise magazines, as well as his monthly Technology for Business column for the Atlanta Tribune, and hosts the popular *Technology For Business $ake* radio program.

Meet David Bullock

David Bullock is President and Managing Director of White Bullock Group, Inc, a business development firm.

David is a degreed mechanical engineer with a thorough understanding of process control. A switch to sales resulted in over $100 million worth of goods and services sold in a seven-year period.

The process design and sales experience came together in his work with Dr. James Kowalick as a certified TRIZ/Taguchi Ad Optimization Specialist.

David has created very effective combinations of processes that lead to increased sales by up to 300%. His unique approach and proven success have made him an authority among internet marketing and business development experts.

David has been featured in Black Enterprise Magazine and Direct Marketing News. He served as Technical Editor for The Adwords for Dummies book. Also, he is a regular contributor The NetEffect Magazine. Recently, David was recognized as one of the *50 Most Powerful and Influential Men in Social Media.*

Brent Leary and David Bullock

Timeline

The Story Inside The Story

June 2008
Reworked Template and Setup Blog

July 2008

July 30, 2008
Official Launch of Barack20.com

July 31, 2008
Blog post: The Senator, Twitter and You

Reposting of video, edited audio and text

August 2008

August 5, 2008
Start of Podcast Updates

August 27, 2008
Democratic National Convention

Interview on WURD 900am Philadelphia

SlideShare Obama2.0 Presentation Moved To First Page

September 2008

Sept 2008
Atlanta Tribune - The Revolution Will Be Twitterized

Sept 8, 2008
Inbound Marketing Summit

Sept 20-21, 2008
Blog World Expo

October 2008

October 8, 2008
SCORE Atlanta Sales and Marketing conference

October 14, 2008
A Conversation with The Tech Team Behind BarackObama.com

October 18, 2008
Barcamp Nashville
David Bullock Presents
Case Study Findings To Nashville Audience

Oct 20, 2008
Shelbyville Times-Gazette:
Story: Campaign goes the high-tech route
BlackEnterprise Article
SlideShare Obama2.0 Presentation Moved To First Page

Inc.com - Barack 2.0
(http://blog.inc.com/technology/2008/10/barack_20.html)

November 2008

Nov 3, 2008
University of Va Webinar
Video interview http://www.youtube.com/watch?v=3M9vGI6hSWE

Nov. 26, 2008
LA Times
(http://latimesblogs.latimes.com/washington/2008/11/obama

Election Month
Book Creation
Speaking Engagements

December 2008

December 2008
Book Release And Promotion
Speaking Engagements

Brent Leary and David Bullock

Engaged, Empowered & Mobilized

What Your Business Can Learn from the
Obama Campaign's Interactive Media Strategy

by

Graduate Students: Loren Bale, Caroline Dahllöf, Lee Jelenic

Wharton Interactive Media Initiative

May, 2009

This paper was written as the final project for Marketing 768: Monetizing Emerging Interactive Media.

"Indeed, in any discussion of the 2008 presidential race, it's important to stipulate this fact right up front: in any prior year, Barack Obama would have lost. Here was a junior senator, a relatively-unknown black politician running against the most established, powerful, and well-financed Democratic machine in modern history: the Clinton family. So how did a man just four years removed from the Illinois State Senate catapult himself to the White House in a landslide and defeat two of politics' best-known brands, Hillary Clinton and John McCain? How did he pull off a staggering margin of nearly 200 electoral votes and 8.5 million popular votes and win nine states George W. Bush took in 2004?"[i]

-Garrett Graff, Editor at Washingtonian Magazine

"If anyone still doubts whether New Media Marketing is something they should take advantage of for their business, just look at Barack's win and ask yourself, can I afford NOT to use new media to get the word out for my business, platform, or campaign?"[ii] (This quote appears inside the cover of Barack 2.0 by David Bullock and Brent Leary)

-Debora Cole Micek, Founder of BLOGi360.com – TribalSeduction.com

If web 2.0's new Interactive Media can be defined at all, it is: an accelerator, an enabler, an equalizer, and above all, a mobilization tool.

In this merciless business world of 2009, companies don't linger for multiple years, slowly burning cash and teetering between success and failure. To survive, companies must collaborate with their customers to innovate and develop new products. It is a place where accountability is paramount and transparency is the norm. It is, in short, a place where a man can go from being virtually unknown to achieving the most powerful position in the world - in just four years.

While there are plenty of intriguing stories about young companies using new media (or even old-line companies that have shifted their focus to new media) there is no company, organization, movement, or individual that has better utilized interactive media than the Obama Campaign. This campaign changed the political game forever by using new and interactive media as the foundation for their entire strategy. This enabled them to organize and execute standard political campaign processes light years faster than any historical benchmark. Doing so on a scale previously **unimaginable**:

> *"When we turned to the community, they were there. We sent staff into Colorado and Missouri for caucuses, and the staff was already half-organized." The theme of the campaign, direct from Obama, was that the people <u>were</u> the organization. "We were there to support the people," Plouffe continues, "but that simply would not have been possible if we did not have a set of online tools that enabled us to do that. It wasn't just a tactic. Chris made that happen."* [iii]

> -Obama Campaign Manager David Plouffe, quoted in Fast Company Magazine, discussing how Facebook Co-Founder Chris Hughes utilized social media to organize offline campaign events.

The Obama campaign shattered the mold for every major measureable campaign statistic, especially the three that matter the most: volunteers, money-raised, and votes garnered.

Thinking back to early 2004, before Obama's nationally televised speech at the Democratic Convention, it would be impossible to fathom him ascending to the Oval Office in four years. Democrats Hillary Clinton, John Edwards, John Kerry, and Howard Dean had all spent considerable time building their political brand in the national spotlight. In addition, all of them had extensive political experience and connections compared to Barack Obama, a man who was only then running to be a first-term Senator for Illinois. On the Republican side two nationally recognizable names were considered favorites for the 2008 election: John McCain, a war hero and fixture in American politics for over three decades; And Rudy Giuliani, the man who became a household name in the 1990's for cleaning up New York City, and "America's Mayor" during the 9/11 tragedy.

So how is it possible that Barack Obama was able to surpass all of these great politicians in such a short time? The answer is that his team embraced and leveraged interactive media with a cross-platform, cross-channel strategy like no organization had ever done before.

Whether or not you agree with Barack Obama's politics, it is hard not to respect and even like the man. The reason for this is that as Americans, we feel like we *know* him. The truth is we do, we know him better than we have ever known a President or presidential candidate. This is no accident. Both the McCain and Clinton campaigns used interactive media, but the major difference between their campaigns and Obama's is that interactive media was simply a tactic, or one spoke in their wheel. For the Obama campaign it was **THE MAJOR STRATEGY** and the hub of the wheel. Unlike the two aforementioned campaigns that viewed interactive media as just another channel to disseminate policy, or worse, to experiment with their alter egos, the Obama campaign took it to another level by using it to give Americans a chance to know the candidate as a person, a father, and a Facebook-friend...all while maintaining a consistent and authentic message.

In this piece, we offer a case by case analysis of how the Obama campaign used interactive media to raise more money, gain more volunteers, and ultimately receive more votes than his major competition. A closer look at the national popular vote and some of the most narrowly-contested States helps put the sheer size advantage of Obama's new media initiative in perspective displaying how vital it was to paving his path to 1600 Pennsylvania Avenue[iv]:

Popular and Electoral Vote Totals

	Obama	McCain
Popular Vote	69,297,997 (52.9%)	59,597,520 (45.5%)
Total Electoral Votes	365	173

Most Narrow Obama State Victories by Popular Vote

State	Electoral Votes	Obama Votes	McCain Votes	Obama Victory Margin
North Carolina	15	2,142,651	2,128,474	14,177
Indiana	11	1,374,039	1,345,648	28,391
New Hampshire	4	384,826	316,534	68,292

Most Narrow Obama State Victories by % of Popular Vote (Excluding NC and IN since they are displayed above)

State	Electoral Votes	Obama % of Vote	McCain % of Vote	Obama Victory Margin
Florida	27	51%	48.2%	2.8%
Ohio	20	51.5%	46.9%	4.6%

Through our research, we developed six major conclusions, or "six rules of new media" that can be universally applied to any new media strategy in business or politics:

1) **Interactive Media is NOT an extension of the proverbial soapbox, but *it IS* a platform to mobilize people:** Before any organization embarks on a new media strategy, it must define a purpose beyond boardroom buzzwords like "generate awareness" and "drive engagement." Interactive media should *only* be used with a defined purpose - one that involves mobilizing users towards an action. For Proctor and Gamble this purpose is product development via their customer ecosystem. For Ford Motor, it is currently collaborating with "agents" to bring new product experiences to their network. For the Obama campaign this included organizing, fund raising, and ultimately voting. The downside of failing to identify a purpose is that in this "new reality," a brand that took years to build can be severely damaged with a single poor new media execution. *Case in point:* Wrigley launched a seemingly aimless 2009 strategy to replace their homepage with various trendy new media interfaces like Twitter and Wikipedia. This resulted in a lack of brand control where site visitors must provide their age before entering and the following can be seen:

 User: i eat rainbows and s**t **skittles!**
34 minutes ago from *web* · Reply · View Tweet

^v *from www.skittles.com/chatter.htb*

v

From what we saw, the above message was only moderate on the potentially offensive scale.

But it's still very dangerous for a brand with such a low customer switching cost. Sour Patch Kids anyone?

Be careful, however. Simply defining a purpose and calling to action will not ensure a home run. In early 2009 Burger King launched *The Whopper Sacrifice* on Facebook, which incentivized individuals to de-friend ten people in order to receive a coupon for a free hamburger. The campaign was suspended shortly after launch because it violated a specific Facebook policy.^{vi} Brand Republic estimates that more that 230,000 people were de-friended, which translates to over 23,000 free hamburgers.^{vii} Although we applaud Burger King's outside-the-box thinking and definitive call to action, it seems risky to potentially offend 230,000 people just to make 23,000 happy.

Brent Leary and David Bullock

2) **Execution trumps early adoption:** Being the first industry player to adopt new media as a strategy is not imperative; there is no cost for users to befriend, follow someone or something new. Doing it right is much more important than doing it *first*; there is a personal cost for users to receive irrelevant information. It's important to note that social media has been used before in presidential campaigns [See Exhibit 2] as Dean supporters used meetup.com to organize events. John McCain utilized a very successful website in the 2000 primary. The Obama Campaign advantage was not the speed in which they adopted social media but their *execution* across every platform, which was vastly superior to any comparable campaign. Although a small first-mover advantage exists, social media is a long-term investment and not a quick fix. Remember, creating a community takes time, especially when its purpose is to help build a brand.

3) **Consistency across channels, platforms, and even offline is vital to a successful strategy:** Despite the seemingly infinite new media channels to choose from, the message must be consistent and clear across all. Too often a brand views new media as an opportunity to show another dimension that ultimately confuses customers or contradicts the true value proposition. The other danger in a lack of consistency across channels is that a consumer who only utilizes one specific new media channel will have a very skewed sense of the brand. During the 2008 campaign, John McCain's Twitter page was mostly used for 140 character "micro attacks." This posturing contradicted his reputation for operating clean campaigns and respecting his opponents and could have seriously skewed the opinion of a Gen-Y voter who used Twitter as his/her primary election information center. Interestingly, after the election John McCain created a new very successful twitter account, which offers a much more balanced and seemingly authentic thread of the Senator's daily engagements.

4) **Authenticity is like oxygen, without it, your interactive media strategy will suffocate:** In the age of Google, YouTube, and Facebook it is easier than ever to check your facts and hold people accountable. Generation-Y is very good at this. Generation-X is catching on. The moment your brand positions itself in a way that is inconsistent with the brand that Gen-Y or Gen-X has come to know, they call you on it, and then shut you off. Case in point:

In late September 2007 Bill Clinton sent an e-mail to Hillary supporters titled: <u>You, me, a TV, and a bowl of chips.</u> The e-mail announced a contest where three winners would be selected to watch a Democratic debate in the company of Bill Clinton.

Two days later, Hillary Clinton sent a follow-up e-mail: "Can I ask you a favor, Bill mentioned a big bowl of chips in the e-mail he sent you on Tuesday. If you are one of the three people who get the chance to join him, can you make sure he eats carrots, not chips?"[viii]

This e-mail exchange was a gross miscalculation of the intelligence of the voting public. It implied an affectionately bantering husband-and-wife schtick that the public might find hard to swallow.

Regardless of the current state of the Clinton's relationship, there probably wasn't a single 2008 voter in the US that didn't remember the Monica Lewinsky scandal, with most of the voters even remembering names like Gennifer Flowers and Paula Jones. Given the "Google" levels of transparency in the new media world, businesses and companies can no longer "sweep bad memories under the rug" and pretend they never happened. This was a severe violation of the new media rule of authenticity, and it was not an isolated mistake for the Clinton campaign.

5) **The conversation must be "two-way," otherwise your message will be filtered as white noise:** Web 2.0 has enabled "The Conversation" to happen, but the two caveats are: your brand, company, or organization must be worthy of attention and you must be willing to listen as much as you speak. David Bullock and Brent Leary showcase a primary-season snapshot comparison between Hillary Clinton and Barack Obama on Twitter in their book **Barack Obama's Social Media Lessons for Business.** In it, they discuss the following:

	Obama	Clinton
Followers	44,596	4,164
Following	46,252	0
Updates	147	175

Twitter statistics from Bullock and Leary[ix]

With Obama it is a two-way conversation (he is actually following more than is following him). Even if he and his team aren't listening to everyone, it *appears* that they are. This seems like simple blocking and tackling, but the Clinton political machine didn't figure this out until it was too late. Clinton actually has more updates, but given her significantly smaller audience, she is getting much less bang for her effort buck.[x]

6) **"Viral" is NOT a viable and controllable strategy, but rather it is the exponential web 2.0 effect of a well executed campaign:** The Obama campaign created a strong brand by being authentic and consistent across all channels and genuinely engaging in a two-way conversation. As a result, user-generated content (UGC) exploded virally and ultimately helped strengthen the brand. The danger of not executing new media rules 3, 4, & 5 is that the users generating the content may ultimately damage the brand, or simply have no incentives to produce UGC.

Applying an Old Theory

From a theoretical standpoint, the best way to compare the Obama Campaign's interactive media performance to that of his rivals is to apply the underlying principles of Gross Rating Points (GRP). GRP is the sum of ratings achieved by a specific media vehicle or the percentage of a target audience reached by an advertisement[xi]. It is used to evaluate the performance of traditional advertisements. Although it is generally used to measure a single advertisement, GRP utilizes two important dimensions: **Reach** and **Frequency**. Although web 2.0 is infinite in its measurable dimensions, applying a reach and frequency philosophy can simplify the analysis. Executing well and preaching a consistent message in an authentic manner (all while engaging in a two-way conversation across as many web 2.0 channels as possible) is the only way to maximize the **Reach** and **Frequency** of the message. In other words, if a business or organization follows the first five aforementioned "rules," then it's **Reach** and **Frequency** will be maximized.

Obama used the various new media channels to maximize his scope and reach even to those who preferred only one new media channel. The **Reach** component can be maximized by executing a broad media effort across all appropriate web 2.0 channels. McCain and Clinton performed close to par with Obama in this category. It was along the **Frequency** axis that the Obama Campaign vastly outperformed the competition.

Obama's message was consistent (rule #3) regardless of which new media channel it occupied. The same cannot be said for McCain and Clinton. The consistency in his content suggests that the campaign assumed people could understand the message even if they only consumed it via a single new media channel. While some individuals depend heavily on only one channel, most consume multiple channels, which meant that voters received the same ideology from Obama across multiple channels, maximizing his **Frequency.** Both McCain and Clinton used different channels for different means (i.e. Twitter was one of McCain's main "attack" channels, while Clinton used Twitter to appear informal and "chatty."[xii]) The result was that regardless of which channel Obama content was consumed, the branding and message was identical—the same cannot be said for his rivals.

The following is data that represents Obama's superior **Reach x Frequency** performance over Hillary Clinton during the democratic primary season:

Tale of the Tape
(March 2008)

iii compete

			Edge	Margin
FaceTime Share	78%	21%	Obama	4:1
Wikipedia Article Readers	280,000	62,000	Obama	4:1
Website Visitors	2,010,000	1,050,000	Obama	2:1
Share of Pennsylvania Web Visitors (as of 4/8/08)	65%	35%	Obama	2:1
Hours Spent on YouTube Channel	539,000	53,100	Obama	10:1
Money Raised in March	$40,000,000	$20,000,000	Obama	2:1

Compete.com statistics for media exposure during Democratic primary[xiii]

Since the calculation of GRP is a function of **Reach x Frequency**, one can see how important a consistent and authentic strategy can be to web 2.0 marketing performance. What sets *web 2.0 GRP* apart from *traditional GRP* is the existence of viral trends and the blogosphere. The greater the *web 2.0 GRP*, the more fuel for both bloggers and UGC creators to continue spreading the message, which has an *exponential* effect. The caveats are that the branding must be clear (rule #3-consistency & #4-authenticity) so that the "viral" message maintains the brand mantra, while the conversation must be two-way (rule #5) so that users feel compelled to develop content and "participate."

We propose that the web 2.0 version of the standard GRP function is: (Reach x Frequency)$^{Reach \times Frequency}$, where the exponent represents the power that viral marketing and bloggers can have on the success of a campaign. One can see it is theoretically dependent on the original **Reach** and **Frequency,** and then compounded exponentially by that very metric. In short, if you execute **Reach** and **Frequency** well, then the bloggers and UGC creators will take the message to another level *for* you.

If every new media channel and platform represents a spoke in a wheel, then www.barackobama.com represents the hub of the wheel. Although the Obama Campaign used each channel to communicate a message, the underlying purpose was to drive traffic back to his own website. This site worked to connect and mobilize an army of volunteers and supporters ("customers") like none other in history. This very same concept can be transferred and applied to any business.

Web Video

Outside of www.barackobama.com, YouTube was the central component of the Obama Campaign web video strategy. Unlike many current companies trying to harness the viral power of YouTube and the web video phenomenon, the Obama Campaign understood that "going viral" cannot be a stand-alone strategy, but instead is the result of a successful strategic implementation (Rule #6). The campaign wanted to take full advantage of the cost-free UGC and viral aspects of YouTube, but also wanted to exert a certain level of control on the content. For this reason they launched their own YouTube page on September 5, 2006. The URL is www.youtube.com/user/barackobamadotcom and the power behind this prong of the Obama new media machine is staggering. Obama's YouTube channel debuted *first*...five months before his official campaign site and months before his official campaign announcement! This order emphasizes how very central web video was to this mission.

The two facets of the Obama YouTube page indicating the strategic lens in which the campaign (and now the administration) view this tool are...

1) That its use did not end when the campaign ended. In fact, Obama still regularly uploads videos that serve as an explanation of policy and as a call to action for Americans.

2) That there are currently (04/2009) 169,888[xiv] subscribers to this channel accounting for a total of 21,373,781 channel views. Given that a high majority of the Obama content uploaded to this channel is footage that was made for other media outlets (i.e. his website, speeches, interviews, and television ads), the campaign was able to utilize this free channel to serve both recycled, original, and user-generated content to another 169,888 people.

As of 4/10/2009 there were 1,838 Obama videos on the YouTube channel. The top five are as follows:

Video/Description	Origin Date	Video Length	YouTube Views	Text Comments
Barack Obama on Ellen DeGeneres Show	October 2007	1:25	6,947,926	1,661
Speech on Race and Politics	March 2008	37:39	5,975,188	10,046
Election Day Victory Speech in Chicago	November 2008	17:01	4,807,140	0
"Yes We Can" Speech in NH	January 2008	13:09	2,819,784	1,520
Iowa Caucus Victory Speech	January 2008	14:07	2,363,586	5,324

[xv]

Despite the negative connotation given to the word "leverage" during the recent financial crisis, when applied correctly, leverage can be an integral part of a winning new media strategy. Two of the four definitions cited for "leverage" on www.dictionary.com are descriptive of the role YouTube and other web video played in the Obama Campaign strategy:

1. Power or ability to act or to influence people, events, decisions, etc.; sway

2. The use of a small initial investment, credit, or borrowed funds to gain a very high return in relation to one's investment, to control a much larger investment..[xvi]

Combine these definitions into one meaning in the context of the power of YouTube within the Obama Campaign, and the strategy becomes clear. To upload an original video to YouTube requires nothing more than a camera and a computer. To upload an existing video to YouTube requires only the video file, a computer and an internet connection. From a dollar standpoint it was extremely cheap for Obama to create videos where he could speak directly to his followers.[xvii]

YouTube also represented a place where the campaign and its supporters could deposit high quality and more expensive footage that was shot on someone else's budget. By using YouTube to recycle the best Obama footage, the campaign truly maximized the use of every minor investment it and other media outlets and users made (i.e. CNN), thus truly *leveraging* this content.

There have been few presidential candidates with as broad a personal appeal as Barack Obama...and the facts support this. True, he is a compelling individual. But he is arguably no more compelling than many other individuals who ran for President. The major difference between Obama and his political rivals was his campaign's ability to clearly communicate his brand character and message. This ensured that the voting public understood not only his policy, but his personality. Once established, this branding remained consistent (rule #3).

Case in point; the most popular video on his YouTube page (with almost 7 million views) was not a speech on economic, foreign, or environmental policy. In fact, it was a one-minute-and twenty-five-second clip of Obama appearing on the Ellen DeGeneres show from October of 2007. Over half of the video shows Obama entering the show and literally busting a move to Beyonce's "Crazy in Love," then he strolls over to a speed bag and registers a textbook left hook that hits the bag so hard it knocks his watch off.[xviii]

It is hard to imagine John McCain or Hillary Clinton pulling off the same entrance! But the point is not whether they actually could - the point is that even if they did, their campaigns weren't leveraging that type of content in a completely free channel so that it could be viewed another 7 million times and commented on 1,661 times after the original airing.

YouTube gave Obama a critical mass content platform outside of his own website. YouTube's comment section also provided an arena for total engagement between Obama's supporters.

Finally, by heavily emphasizing YouTube in addition to his own website, the Obama campaign placed their candidate directly in Google's Search Engine Optimization (SEO) crosshairs. In MKTG 768, countless guest speakers (as well as Wharton Interactive Media Initiative (WIMI) Director Steve Ennen) have emphasized the importance of "winning with Google" in order to be relevant in the web 2.0 arena. Given that Google purchased YouTube in October 2006 for $1.65 Billion in cash, industry experts David Bullock and Brent Leary agree that it is a safe assumption that Google has wired YouTube to be extremely relevant in its search engine.[xix]

The Competition

Without benchmarking relevant competitors, it is hard to truly comprehend how advanced Obama's web video strategy actually was. Here is a detailed up to date data comparison between John McCain's YouTube channel and Barack Obama's:

As of 4/10/2009	Obama	McCain
Launched	9/5/2006	2/23/2007
Still Active	Yes	Yes
Total Videos	1,838	329
Subscribers	167,973	28,158
Total Video Views to Date	21,230,955	2,340,013
Views for Most Viewed Video	6,947,926	2,254,776

The official McCain YouTube channel address is: www.youtube.com/user/JohnMcCaindotcom

While the drastic data differences between the sites tells a compelling tale of performance, reach and frequency, it also indicates the level of priority for web video within the two campaigns. Most importantly, the differentiation between the site content indicates how differently the campaigns viewed the web video opportunity and the potential viral externality:

- McCain's 329 videos are mostly a compilation of serious campaign speeches and attack ads. There are very few videos that would appeal to anyone who isn't a political junkie and there are definitely no videos showing McCain gyrating his hips with Ellen DeGeneres or other introspective looks into the man. Simply put: Obama's video content appeals to a much broader audience. The drastic difference between Obama and McCain's YouTube numbers are even more relevant given that the popular vote differential was relatively close with 66,862,039 votes for Obama to 58,318,442 for McCain. Phrased another way, Obama only won battleground states like North Carolina and Indiana by popular vote margins of 13,692 and 25,836 respectively. This fully legitimizes Obama's efforts to attract 167,973 YouTube subscribers versus McCain's 28,158
- It is clear that the McCain camp learned from the Obama camp. Although he is not President, John McCain is still a relevant leader in this country, and like Obama, he has kept his YouTube channel active since the end of the election.
- Obama & McCain both offered code so users could embed the YouTube channel in their websites

Show Me the Money! (... and the Volunteers)

In addition to "potential votes garnered", two other metrics weigh the effects of YouTube. These are: "money donated" and "volunteers recruited."

The hub in any campaign's wheel is its website. That is where donors can make payments and volunteers can sign up. Every other interactive media initiative includes the goal of driving traffic back to the website. While Search Engine Optimization (SEO) can be an effective way to direct this traffic, YouTube provides a special way to appeal to potential donors and volunteers that aren't normally driving their search engine towards political websites. Both McCain and Obama's YouTube channel clearly point to their campaign websites, but Obama used YouTube to drive and convert a broader audience which no doubt included many new and previously politically uninvolved individuals. Meanwhile, McCain's YouTube channel was only attracting his mainstream followers and political junkies

Contrasting the two YouTube channels reaffirms that interactive media was only a tactic for the McCain camp while it was a full-fledged strategy for the Obama campaign. McCain broke three important *rules of new media strategy:*

1) He used YouTube as an extension of his soapbox (violation of new media rule #1), filling it with speeches and attack ads. He did not leveraging the chance to *reach* new voters, direct them to his site, and *mobilize* them.

2) He failed to engage in a two-way conversation via other channels (Twitter and texting), thus his supporters never felt compelled to carry a "viral" movement in the same fashion as the Obama voters (violation of new media rules #5 and #6).

Viral Video: Obama Girl and YouBama

If there is one facet of the Obama Campaign execution that the Baby-Boomer-laden-executive-leadership teams in corporate America should learn, it's that viral success *is* an "effect" of a well executed new media strategy. *It is not* a stand-alone strategic initiative (see new media rule #6).

By implementing a cross channel multi-platform new media strategy, the Obama campaign sought to organize and engage an army of supporters who were willing to donate, volunteer, and vote. By doing this well and backing it up with a consistent message that inspired people, the campaign achieved the natural positive externality of web 2.0: *viral marketing*. (By definition, viral marketing occurs when independent individuals take it upon themselves to advocate for an organization or brand with which they have no affiliation. Two of the best examples of viral marketing that occurred as a result of an excellent new media strategy are Obama Girl and YouBama.)

Obama Girl: Barely Political and almost baring it all

At one time or another during 2008, most Americans heard of the Obama Girl phenomenon. It was hard to watch a late night talk show or prime time CNN election coverage without at least a passing referral. On June 13th, 2007 Ben Relles (founder of www.barelypolitical.com) posted a video on YouTube of Amber Lee Ettinger in a music video titled "Crush on Obama"

(www.youtube.com/watch?v=wKsoXHYICqU&feature=channel_page).

Aside from being provocative, sexy, catchy, and original, the video is actually somewhat insightful and offers a unique perspective as to why Obama was an attractive candidate for generation's X & Y. The video has gotten over 13 million views and over 73,000 comments and was followed by another 70 videos starring Ettinger.

It is hard to quantify how beneficial this momentum was to the Obama movement, but there is no doubt that a franchise built around an attractive and scantily clad young female and her strong emotional attachment to Barack Obama yielded extremely positive ancillary benefits, especially among young and previously uninvolved individuals.

YouBama: The Citizen generated Campaign[xx]

The "About Us" tab on www.youbama.com explains the site and its purpose:

> The goal of YouBama is to democratize the election campaign process. All content is generated by citizens and voted on by citizens.
>
> Think about it as the unofficial presidential campaign for Barack Obama. Voters can say what they want, how they want. Then they vote on the videos so the best ones rise to the top.
>
> This site was created by two Stanford University students. We have no connection to the official Obama campaign. We have no sponsors or group affiliations. The site was built using open source software.
>
> If you have any questions or comments please send an email to:
>
> contact@youbama.com
>
> Upload a video and join the campaign today![xxi]

[xxii]

Youbama is another example of the positive externalities that companies and organizations can expect when they successfully execute a new media strategy for a strong brand. The Obama

Campaign engaged in a consistent, authentic, two-way conversation from the beginning (see new media rules #3, #4 and #5), thus his supporters felt compelled to develop more ways to continue the conversation among themselves.

The most popular video on this site is a 37 minute video of Obama's speech on racial equality shortly after the Reverend Wright scandal reached its peak. The video has almost 6 million views. As an example of the type of scope a viral movement can offer, the second most popular video is a three minute music video by Black Eyed Peas front-man, Will. I. Am titled "We Are The Ones." This video has 3.5 million views to date.

McCain and Clinton's Antiviral issues

By breaking down the new media strategies of the McCain and Clinton campaigns, it is clear why their supporters never developed a "www.YouCain.com" or why a "Clinton Boy" never took the web video world by storm. Their campaigns were either inconsistent in message/character portrayal (McCain turning into an attack dog and Hillary Clinton trying to portray a loving marriage) or one-way in their communication (Clinton did not follow anybody on Twitter); further violations of new media rules #3, #4, and #5. These new media missteps handcuffed their supporter's ability to continue the conversation amongst themselves with viral activities.

A final quote from a recent article summarizes the campaign's video results and highlights their ability to respond to customer needs, providing further proof that the "two-way conversation" was a reality:

> *All told, the campaign created nearly 2,000 YouTube videos, which in turn were watched for some 14.6 million hours, according to a study by TubeMogul.com. This multitude of videos, Graham-Felson explains, was part of a broad micro-targeting effort whereby each video was aimed at speaking to a particular group of voters or supporters. Those efforts paid off in a big way: TubeMogul estimated that Obama received the equivalent of some $45 million in "free" television airtime from people watching those videos. One of the surprising lessons from the campaign, Rospars and Graham-Felson say, was that people wanted longer cuts. "In the beginning we were just posting clips, but people kept commenting they wanted the whole thing," Rospars says.[xxiii]*

> - Sam Graham-Felson was the Obama Campaign's lead blogger and Joe Rospars was the campaign's online director. This excerpt is from an article written by *Washingtonian Magazine* editor Garrett Graff.

Podcasts

It should be noted that John McCain, Hillary Clinton, Barack Obama, and many other presidential candidates effectively used video and audio podcasts to showcase their best policy speeches. These podcasts are offered in multiple mediums with the most popular channel being iTunes.

David Bullock and Brent Leary point out that this is a medium in which a candidate or company spokesman can be almost *guaranteed* a captive audience, when you consider the way in which this media is usually consumed: headphones. Interestingly, during the campaign this media content seemed much more controlled, and positioned for the passionate political follower. What set Obama's use of podcasts ahead of his competition was simply that his podcast persona and message remained consistent with his other media channels, compared to the contradictions and inconsistencies of voice that McCain and Clinton displayed across the various channels. [for a picture of Obama's iTunes podcast page, see Exhibit 3]

Blogs

The Blogosphere is equally as misunderstood among corporate America's baby-boomer-executive-leaders as is the concept of "going viral." Like viral marketing, brand success in the blogosphere is a positive externality resulting from a well-executed new media strategy [part of the exponential portion of (Reach x Frequency)$^{\text{Reach x Frequency}}$]. Executing well and preaching a consistent message in an authentic manner while engaging in a two-way conversation is akin to providing fuel for the blogosphere's proverbial fire. The Obama Campaign maximized these new media inputs across a variety of channels, thus providing bloggers multiple access points to all of the information. Both the superior **Reach** and **Frequency** of Obama's message resulted in a greater blogosphere following than either of his rivals.

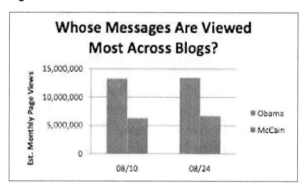

Monthly page views across syndicated blogs from TechCrunch[xxiv]

Social Networks

On Obama's campaign webpage he has a section called "Obama Everywhere" where he lists sixteen social networks he belongs to. Looking through his profiles on the different networks we see the following trends;

1) Regardless of social network, the whole profile is complete.

2) He creates groups whenever possible. For example, on LinkedIn he has *Obama for America*, on Facebook he has *Students for Obama* among many others.

3) He has links to his other platforms whenever possible, creating a tightly knit web that is difficult to escape. For example, on MySpace he is linked to YouTube, Facebook, LinkedIn, iTunes, Flickr, and Digg.

4) He uses a combination of text, images and videos in his posts.

By being equally dedicated to large social networks, (i.e. Facebook, LinkedIn, MySpace) as he is to niche networks where he might only have a few hundred friends (which is the case with Glee) he comes off as authentic (new media rule #4). He portrays an image of wanting to connect and build relationships with the communities rather than simply promote his brand.

McCain did not have the same success with social networks. Although he belongs to many of the same networks as Obama, he was unable build similarly sized groups. We feel the main reason for this failure is that his effort was not authentic (violation of new media rule #4). On many niche networks he either did not complete his profile or only joined the network in the final hours of the election (e.g. McCain joined BlackPlanet.com only a few weeks before the November election). His lack of interest in building a relationship with the niche communities not only prevented him from gaining followers on the specific networks, but may also have had negative implications on his larger networks as most people belong to more than one network.

Brent Leary and David Bullock

The key takeaway is that the effort of building relationship with a community must be consistent (new media rule #3) whether in a large general network or a niche network. Without consistency, the efforts appear unauthentic (new media rule #4) and can have a negative spillover effect on other networks. Social media is a long-term investment: Obama recognized this and used it accordingly [see exhibit 5] while McCain appears to have used it as a quick fix [see exhibit 6].

Text Messaging

The purpose of the Obama Campaign text messages were to mobilize people to act — register to vote, organize events for the campaign, and ultimately vote.[xxv] An example text message read:

> "Help Barack. Tell your friends & family the last day to register to vote in CA is this Monday, Oct 20th! Visit VoteForChange.com to register NOW. Please forward." [xxvi]

They utilized no negative campaigning and no fundraising on this platform. It focused on action messages that people received two or three times per week. In September of 2008, Obama localized his text messages allowing the campaign to send location specific messages such as asking for volunteers from neighboring states and informing about local events and voting deadlines.[xxvii]

People could opt-in by texting HOPE to 62262 or on barackobama.com. The campaign used two additional tactics to collect phone numbers;

(1) they asked for voters' cell numbers at registration drives[xxviii]

(2) they created the campaign "Be the First to Know" (my.barackobama.com/page/s/firsttoknow). The premise of this campaign was that Obama would let "you" be the first to know (by text message) his choice for VP before a public announcement was made as long as you "opted in" and provided your cell phone number. The campaign not only used a standard presidential campaign event (announcing VP) to mass collect cell phone numbers, but also strengthened the personal bond with the voters and generated media buzz.

According to Aaron Strauss and Allison Dale,[xxix] text messages increased voter turnout by 3.1% among newly registered voters because the messages reminded voters of deadlines. Strauss and Dale also say that 59% of people found the text messages helpful. Another study[xxx] shows that text-based get-out-the-vote appeals won one voter for every 25 people contacted. Given that each vote garnered by a text based get-out-the-vote campaign costs $1.50 compared to the historically most efficient get-out-the-vote method of door-to-door visits, which garners 1 vote per 14 visited but cost $29 per new vote, the text channel appears significantly more effective.[xxxi]

The main reason for the effectiveness of this platform is that currently people do not receive an abundant number of text messages relative to other mediums like e-mail. For many, this channel is clear and free of noise, however will become less efficient as adoption and penetration increase.

If this platform was so efficient then why didn't it work for the other candidates? While Obama's messages were professional, Hillary's messages were informal and chatty and only sent a few times a month.[xxxii] In other words, she did not try to mobilize her followers (rule #1) and she was not authentic (rule #4). It seemed that she believed the "younger" platform allowed for a more informal or unprofessional approach. Even more out of touch, McCain viewed a texting strategy to be "beneath a presidential candidate" and only sent one text message the entire campaign, a reminder to vote the day before the election.[xxxiii,xxxiv] There is no doubt this strategy hurt both candidates as they witnessed the Obama campaign utilizing their cache of more than 3 million cell phone numbers to send targeted messages in the days leading up to the election.[xxxv]

Twitter

Obama used tweets to inform his followers about his location and current activities, but the tweets almost always included a call-to-action as well. At the end of each tweet a URL allowed for further engagement. The general format used by the campaign looked like this: "*In <city>, <state> doing <x>. Visit <URL>.*" Here is an example:

> *In Fort Collins, CO. At an "Early Vote for Change" rally. Watch it live at my.barackobama.com/l... 5:22 PM Oct 26th, 2008 from web*

By including the URL, Obama connected this platform with his other platforms such as Scribd, YouTube, MySpace, and barackobama.com. But it was also a way for the campaign to measure how engaged the followers were by tracking URL click-throughs.

	Start date	End date	Updates	Followers[xxxvi]	Following[xxxvii]
Obama	04/29/07	12/05/08	262	635,221	635,221
McCain	09/19/08	10/24/08	26	8,882	6,403

Note how much earlier Obama adopted Twitter usage. Overlay the above Twitter performance gap with the fact that Obama had 3 million cell numbers (which he actively used) while McCain sent only one text message during the entire campaign, and the stark strategy differences between the campaigns becomes clear!

Obama's message is clear, consistent, and frequent [See Exhibit 7]. David All, a republican new-media consultant, said that they were "never pointless"[xxxviii]. In contrast, it seems that most of McCain's tweets are mostly negative campaigning. It is clear from the data that his type of communication did not appeal to many people. He had 1.3% of the followers that Obama had.

It seems as though McCain learned from his rival because on January 23rd, 2009 he created a new Twitter identity, with 273 updates and counting. The tweets are now personal, use various formats, many of them do not use capital letters, which makes us believe that McCain himself is tweeting. McCain is now authentic and as a result has 348,394 followers (compared to the less than 10,000 he had during the election).[xxxix]

Mobile WAP Site and iPhone App

The WAP site was released on August 14th, 2008 [See Exhibit 1]. The campaign said it was targeted towards the heavy cell phone users.[xl] It let users get news and connect with friends. It also allowed users to download video, ringtones, and wallpaper.

The campaign released an iPhone application 33 days before the election[xli] [See Exhibit 1]. The application is similar to their mobile website but with extra features to help the user to remind their friends to vote. The campaign tracked the number of calls to see progress and by the afternoon of the day the app was released, 360 people had made 754 calls.[xlii] The application also used the location information of the iPhone to give user location-specific information.

The smart phone strategy is yet another example of the campaign's effort to ensure they are using the right channel of communication to target people. The message is, as always, consistent with the other platforms. And this tool was largely used to mobilize (rule #1).

E-mail

The Obama campaign used email to push messages out to users and draw them into the website and the other digital platforms. First a user's email address would be procured (collected either during their signup on the website or from a traditional donation form). Then Obama would commence a regular dialog, targeting messages and announcements based on profile/demographic information available in each voter's profile. Email was used with increasing frequency over the course of the campaign: initially starting at 1-2 emails per week in the early phase of the primary, it grew into a barrage of 1-2 emails per day at the height of the action in November. As with all of the other digital media platforms, emails were tightly integrated into the overall campaign message and focused on delivering new video communications, important updates, and requests for donations.

Example campaign emails

During the course of the primary and general elections, Obama built an email database that included 13 million addresses, larger than the combined lists of the National Democratic Party, MoveOn.org (a liberal policy advocacy group), and US Senator John Kerry.[xliii] This offered a dramatic reach and allowed Obama to drive traffic through to his core web presence where passive voters could be empowered to become active supporters.

The Queen Bee: BarackObama.com

The internet became a primary source for news and information during the latest presidential election. According to The Pew Research Center, 24% of Americans accessed information on the candidates in the 2008 election, up from 13% in 2004 and 9% in 2000[xliv]. This number jumps to 42% for voters aged 18-42 who regularly use the internet for access to candidate and campaign information. Furthermore, 27% of voters younger than 30, and 37% of voters aged 18-24, used social networks regularly to learn about candidates. Obama and his team identified - early - the importance the web would play in the 2008 election. They brought in talented people and a dedication to an integrated online strategy that would set the stage for two years of campaigning records.

> *"Technology has always been used as a net to capture people in a campaign or cause, but not to organize,"* says Obama campaign manager David Plouffe. *"Chris <Hughes> saw what was possible before anyone else."*[xlv]

> - David Plouffe, Chief Campaign Manager for Barack Obama

Features/Design

BarackObama.com is a full-featured website complete with e-commerce functionality, social networking, and rich media integration. Arriving at BarackObama.com, the site immediately presents the latest piece of news, video of Obama, or other relevant and fresh information. Users have the opportunity to read blogs, watch video, and learn about Obama's most recent activities before moving into a specific sub-domain. The e-commerce engine and the tools that powered online donations formed *donations.barackobama.com,* a sub-domain where as much as 6% of web surfers would go to make donations, buy t-shirts, etc. (shown below). Even more impressive however are the features and capabilities that were implemented in my.barackobama.com where Chris Hughes, chief architect and Facebook co-founder, built an entire social network. Features included all the standard features you would expect such as blogging, video sharing, building a personal profile, and connecting to other members, but he and the team took this social network to the next level.

Because they also built savvy new features never before seen such as do-it-yourself event planning tools, voter registration interface, a polling station locator, communication tools to help people create and find user-sponsored events, tools to design fliers and other marketing materials, discussion forums, and an especially novel online phone banking system. The phone banking system would identify 20 voters thought to be on the fence who shared a similar demographic profile to the caller. The caller could then place calls and the website would walk them in real-time through a script that adapted based on the responses of the person on the phone. The tool lets users share some of the campaign details, help people register to vote, find polling stations, and then would record the outcomes of those calls. Below you can see the dashboard for a user that has made 20 calls, attended 2 events, and raised $200. To encourage further engagement, each user is rated with an activity index (shown below as 1 out of 10).

By not only calling people to action, but providing feedback on their action, the campaign shows a deep understating for new media rule #5, the two-way conversation.

BarackObama.com serves as the landing page for the Barack Obama online presence and funnels users from across Obama's entire online presence to a single collection point from which they are directed to appropriate sub-domains. Hughes himself developed the interface and agonized over the details and features that would be included on the site. Despite being understaffed during the primaries, Hughes and his team had implemented an impressive set of features that drove these early engagement numbers while also providing a powerful call to action for the community of users. Users who ultimately provided the Obama campaign with an army of volunteers.

Interestingly, the Obama campaign learned new media rule #2 the hard way. It wasn't until Obama lost the New Hampshire primary that attention shifted to the potential that the website held and the importance of the social network that was beginning to thrive there. Aware that a protracted national primary battle lay ahead of them, the campaign managers began to hunt for additional support. They were amazed to find that - using the social networking tools available on my.barackobama.com - supporters had already self-organized, planned caucus meetings, and rallied to promote Obama's candidacy in their neighborhoods and communities: "*All of a sudden, it made a difference that we have 60 really organized groups in Kansas, a caucus state. And a hugely active Boise for Obama group,*" Hughes recalls.[xlvi] The website became absolutely critical to Obama's success, first in the primaries and then in the general election as the field was perhaps more competitive than any in recent history.

> "*What's amazing is that Hillary built the best campaign that has ever been done in Democratic politics on the old model – she raised more money than anyone before her, she locked down all the party stalwarts, she assembled an all-star team of consultants and she really mastered this top-down, command-and-control type of outfit. And yet she's getting beaten by this political start-up that is essentially a totally different model of the new politics.*" [xlvii]

> - Peter Leyden, New Politics Institute

> "*Campaign staffers dispatched around the country discovered what the MyBO <my.barackobama.com> community had accomplished. When Jeremy Bird, the official state director, parachuted into Maryland to prep for the Potomac primary on February 12, he was astonished to find a whole field operation at work. 'They had the entire thing set up—an office with seven computers, phone lines, a state structure, county chairs, and meetings every other Saturday. They had even picked their own state director.' Obama won with 57.4% of the vote.*" [xlviii]

> - Jeremy Bird, Obama Campaign Official State Director

> "*As staffers fanned out across the country, MyBO became a key tool for them. 'Everywhere we went, we could plug in a zip code, and a list of really excited volunteers would pop up,' explains Bird. Says Plouffe: 'Indiana? North Carolina? We wouldn't have won those states without the grassroots.*'" [xlix]

> - Jeremy Bird and David Plouffe

Metrics

BarackObama.com has been a success by all the traditional web metrics: reach/unique visitors (breadth) and engagement (depth). As seen below, breadth was high as measured by unique visitors, which peaked immediately before the election at 9M for the month of October, the ideal time for a fury of energy, fund raising, and education about the candidate.

BarackObama.com remained a top 1000 web site as ranked by traffic throughout the months leading up to the election. In fact, by January 2008 Obama owned 27% of share in total traffic to all presidential candidate websites combined (see below). Additionally, and largely due to the social networking tools, the depth of engagement during mid 2008 was particularly high and garnered an equal amount of time per user as CNN (even spiking to ~11min in November 2008, on par with Yahoo!).

Another metric that attempts to measure engagement is pages per visit on which Obama outperformed McCain consistently.

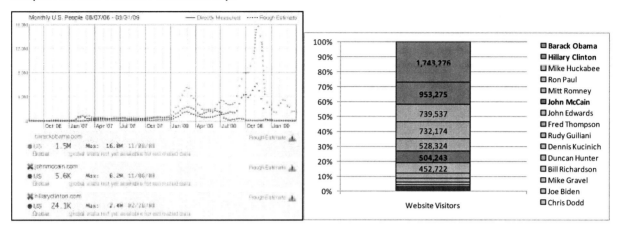

Monthly traffic to candidates' websites[i]

Analysis: share of traffic, Obama has 27% in January 2008[ii]

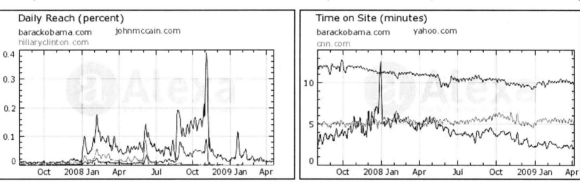

Reach measured as percentage of internet traffic[iii]

Engagement measured by time on site[liii]

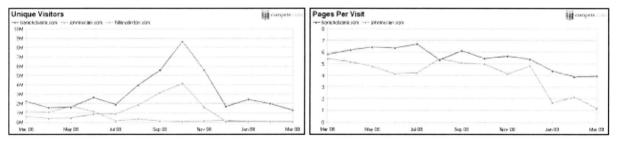

Breadth measured by unique visitors[liv]

Engagement measured by page views per visit[lv]

Barackobama.com managed to both build a strong base of loyal followers, while also maintaining high traffic volume of new users. This balancing act further demonstrates the success of achieving both depth and breadth with the website and the larger digital media platform. The traffic frequency charts (below) demonstrate this marked advantage. While neither candidate has any appreciable "addicts", Obama has a strong core of regular users that produce almost half of the site's normal traffic as compared to McCain's 8% of regular users who produce just one fifth of the traffic (i.e. don't return to the site as often).

The other 52% of traffic visits are generated by 76% of users who are passers-by, representing a broad swatch of new or irregular visitors. McCain on the other hand, has virtually all his visits generated by this passers-by group demonstrating that while he may have attained some breadth, he failed to engage his visitors and build the level of depth that Obama did.

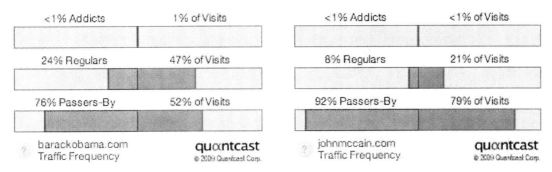

Traffic Frequency from quantcast[lvi]

Addicts are defined as making 30+ visits for a site within 1 month, passers-by are defined as making just once per month, and Regulars are defined as visiting a site between 2 and 30 times per month[lvii].

The types of users that visit BarackObama.com are another important detail in the success of the site and the engagement it was able to drive. The demographic charts below show the characteristics of the traffic that visited each of the candidates' websites. On the left are shown the actual raw demographic breakdowns while the index on the right shows a relative measure of how usual/unusual such a demographic would be against normal web traffic.

Obama's website disproportionally attracted a female audience across a wide range of ages skewing slightly older with a high proportion of high salaried professionals, childless individuals, and African Americans. Such a demographic mix suggests Obama was successful in attracting a relatively diverse group to his campaign, including the full range of ages and women voters. Traffic to McCain's site on the other hand skews towards males at the upper end of the age demographic and Caucasians. This closely matches McCain's personal profile and suggests he was less successful in appealing to a broader audience of voters. Likewise, Hillary's website traffic skews towards women across a variety of ages and ethnic make-ups. Perhaps Hillary was more successful in reaching a broader voter base, but remained challenged to find support amongst male voters.

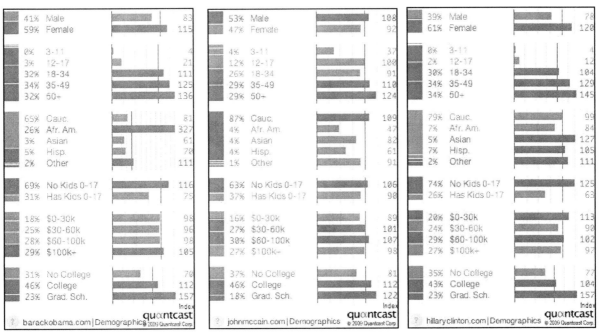

Demographic statistics for Obama[lviii],   McCain[lix],   and Clinton[lx]

Monetizing the Traffic

"74% of wired Obama supporters have gotten political news and information online, compared with 57% of online Clinton supporters. In a head-to-head matchup with internet users who support Republican McCain, Obama's backers are more likely to get political news and information online (65% vs. 56%). Among online Democrats, Obama's supporters are more likely than Clinton's supporters to have made online campaign contributions (17% vs. 8%), to sign online petitions (24% vs. 11%), to have passed along political commentaries in blogs and other forms (23% vs. 13%), and to have watched campaign videos of any kind (64% vs. 43%). Obama's backers are also more likely than McCain's partisans to have engaged in range of online campaign activities." [lxi]

- The Pew Internet and American Life Project

The stats for success by the end of the campaign were staggering and broke new ground for future campaigns. Obama raised three quarters of a billion dollars making this the first-ever billion dollar election (combined total of all presidential candidates' fund raising). At barackobama.com, web visitors created over 2 million profiles, over 200,000 user initiated events were planned through the site and executed across the country, 35,000 community groups were created, 400,000 blogs have been written, and 70,000 personal fund-raising pages netted $30 million.[lxii] The total number of people that contributed online was over 3 million[lxiii] and over 8 million phone calls were placed from the call banking tool.[lxiv] Over 1 million voters were registered to vote through the website, an effort that required just a few staffers working part-time.

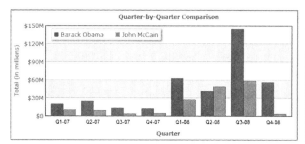

Funds raised by candidates[lxv]

Historical fundraising comparison[lxvi]

In April 2008, Obama raised $31M, 95% of which came via online donations under $200 each vs. Hillary's $20M:

"The Obama team realized that online social networking made physical fundraisers redundant and it also realized that a much better point of entry wasn't $2,300 but less than one-tenth of that: $200. It transformed its website into a social networking zone, and its appeal to the young made this strategy viral." [lxvii]

-Andrew Sullivan, Harvard Ph.D, Sunday Times Political Writer

Obama raised a total of $745M during the election, almost $150M of which was raised in the 3rd quarter of 2008[lxviii]. In fact, a staggering 54% of this dollar figure came from donations under $200, most of which were made on barackobama.com (table below). So great was the volume of online donations, that a Pew Report determined that 8% of internet users had donated money to a candidate online in June 2008 vs. just 3% in 2006.[lxix]

Candidate	Donations ≤$200	Donations $200-$2300	Donations ≥$2300	Donations ≥$4600
Obama, Barack	54%	7%	30%	9%
McCain, John	34%	1%	49%	16%
Nader, Ralph	60%	15%	17%	8%
Barr, Bob	57%	26%	15%	2%
McKinney, Cynthia	34%	56%	10%	0%
Baldwin, Chuck	62%	24%	14%	0%

Percentage of total dollars raised by donation size[lxx]

"During the month of February, for example, his campaign raised a record-setting $55m, $45m of it over the internet without the candidate himself hosting a single fundraiser...And since most have not donated anything like the maximum amount, he doesn't just have a list of names to thank; he has a huge list of names to ask for more. This is a money machine unlike any other." [lxxi]

-Josh Green, political writer for *The Atlantic*

Conclusion

The 2008 election was set to be historic from the outset: only once since the 1920's had an election not included an incumbent or a vice-president. And the election lived up to expectations delivering a fierce battle in which more American voters cast a ballot than ever before in US history.

Barack Obama could not have won the election without the internet-based donations and volunteer mobilization engine he created. Obama and his campaign committee found a way to harness the power of the long-tail and in the process they proved that small donors can carry an election. Obama for America and the entire digital media strategy Obama relied on is potentially *the most successful web 2.0 launch to date anywhere in any industry.*

This historic effort provides insightful lessons that are applicable to businesses, non-profits, and politicians alike:

- Social networking is here to stay. Figure out how your business and goals can tap into this powerful new digital version of social interaction
    1) Actively promote your network's "citizens" to recruit and work for you.
    2) Vast monetization opportunity lies untapped in the long-tail.
- Different people or demographics of people use different communication channels. So in order to communicate with everyone, you need to use *all* of them or risk failing to find everyone.
- Challenge yourself and your organization to experiment with new platforms and maintain your presence there just as seriously as established platforms.
- Go outside the box to hire new media experts (*e.g. Chris Hughes*). Even though Hughes had no political experience, the Obama campaign relied on him to conscript the army of supporters that won the election.
- Finally, whatever business you are in, be sure to utilize our six rules of new media execution:
    1) Interactive Media is *NOT* an extension of the proverbial soap box, but *it IS* a platform to mobilize people.

2) **Execution trumps Early Adoption.**

3) **Consistency across channels, platforms, and offline is vital to a successful strategy.**

4) **Authenticity is like oxygen, without it, your interactive media strategy will suffocate.**

5) **The conversation must be "two-way," otherwlse your message wIll be filtered as white noise.**

6) **"Viral" is NOT a viable and controllable strategy. Instead, it is the exponential web 2.0 effect of a well executed campaign.**

Acknowledgements

We would like to acknowledge David Bullock for many things, the first and foremost being the confirmation that we were not crazy in thinking that a political campaign can be viewed as the ultimate business model in utilizing new media. When we found the book written by David and his partner Brent Leary it invigorated this project and opened an infinite number of doors for us. The most rewarding of these doors was access to David on Twitter [see exhibit 4], E-mail, Skype, and Mobile. He provided countless resources for us and for that we are grateful.

We would also like to thank Steve Ennen: Director of the Wharton Interactive Media Initiative and our instructor in Marketing 768. Steve offered the foundation for examining new media strategies and pushed us to question traditional matrices used in new media. Offering great freedom to explore new media strategies he helped us frame our analysis of the Obama campaign as both a new media strategy as well as the broader business insights the campaign offers.

Authors' Biographies

Loren Bale

Loren recently graduated from The Wharton School with an MBA in Entrepreneurial Management. Loren worked as a management consultant at McKinsey &Company and at PRTM, and as founder of social media site TravelShare.com. Loren holds a bachelor's degree in computer engineering from the University of Toronto.

Caroline Dahllof

Caroline is currently working on the venture, Lyn & Line LLC., that she co-founded in the summer of 2009. The company designs and develops mobile applications. From 1999 to 2007 Caroline worked for Rhythm & Hues Studios, a leader in the visual effects industry. She worked both on the technical and creative side of productions on features such as Superman Returns, Happy Feet, and The Golden Compass. Caroline holds a MBA from The Wharton School of University of Pennsylvania, a MS and BS in computer science from Brown University.

Lee Jelenic

Lee is currently a marketing manager at The Ford Motor Company in Dearborn, Michigan. From 2004-2007, he worked as an equity trader and risk manager at JP Morgan Chase & Co. in New York, NY. Prior to Wall Street, Lee played two seasons of professional hockey, finishing his career playing for the Rochester Americans, an affiliate of the Buffalo Sabres, in the AHL. Lee earned a B.A. degree in Political Science from Yale University in 2001 and an M.B.A. from The Wharton School of The University of Pennsylvania in 2009. At Wharton Lee received his M.B.A. with Honors as a Palmer Scholar for achieving top 5% standing in his class.

APPENDIX

Exhibit 1: Mobile WAP Site and iPhone App

Exhibit 2: Technological Advances in Campaigning

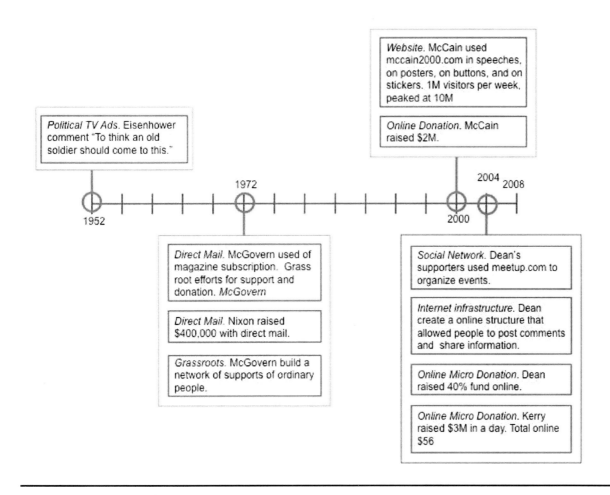

Exhibit 3: Candidate Obama's iTunes Podcast Page

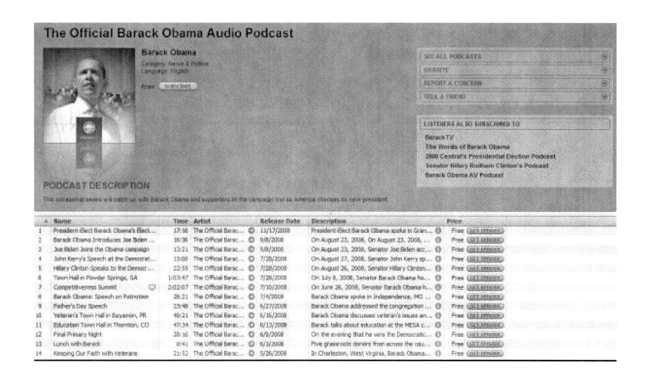

The Official Barack Obama Audio Podcast

Barack Obama
Category: News & Politics
Language: English

Free

PODCAST DESCRIPTION

This successful series will catch up with Barack Obama and supporters on the campaign trail as America chooses its new president.

	Name	Time	Artist		Release Date	Description		Price	
1	President-Elect Barack Obama's Elect...	17:16	The Official Barac...	○	11/17/2008	President-Elect Barack Obama spoke in Gran...	○	Free	
2	Barack Obama Introduces Joe Biden ...	16:36	The Official Barac...	○	9/8/2008	On August 23, 2008, On August 23, 2008, ...		Free	
3	Joe Biden Joins the Obama campaign	13:21	The Official Barac...	○	9/8/2008	On August 23, 2008, Senator Joe Biden acc...	○	Free	
4	John Kerry's Speech at the Democrat...	13:08	The Official Barac...	○	7/28/2008	On August 27, 2008, Senator John Kerry sp...	○	Free	
5	Hillary Clinton Speaks to the Democr...	22:55	The Official Barac...	○	7/28/2008	On August 26, 2008, Senator Hillary Clinton...	○	Free	
6	Town Hall in Powder Springs, GA	1:03:47	The Official Barac...	○	7/28/2008	On July 8, 2008, Senator Barack Obama ho...	○	Free	
7	Competitiveness Summit	2:02:07	The Official Barac...	○	7/10/2008	On June 26, 2008, Senator Barack Obama h...	○	Free	
8	Barack Obama: Speech on Patriotism	28:21	The Official Barac...	○	7/4/2008	Barack Obama spoke in Independence, MO ...	○	Free	
9	Father's Day Speech	23:48	The Official Barac...	○	6/27/2008	Barack Obama addressed the congregation ...	○	Free	
10	Veteran's Town Hall in Bayamon, PR	40:21	The Official Barac...	○	6/16/2008	Barack Obama discusses veteran's issues an...	○	Free	
11	Education Town Hall in Thornton, CO	47:34	The Official Barac...	○	6/13/2008	Barack talks about education at the MESA c...	○	Free	
12	Final Primary Night	28:16	The Official Barac...	○	6/8/2008	On the evening that he wins the Democratic...	○	Free	
13	Lunch with Barack	8:41	The Official Barac...	○	6/3/2008	Five grassroots donors from across the cou...	○	Free	
14	Keeping Our Faith with Veterans	21:52	The Official Barac...	○	5/26/2008	In Charleston, West Virginia, Barack Obama...	○	Free	

Exhibit 4: *From Twitter to E-mail to Mobile in ten minutes:* **A case study within a case study;** *connecting on social media* **(This conversation is a series of direct Tweets between Lee Jelenic and David Bullock, cut from Lee Jelenic's Twitter account, which explains why each snippet shows David's picture.**

Lee reaches out to David with two tweets only days after first meeting David on Twitter:

 davidbullock David, are you interested in a skype call (5 min) to my MBA class during my Wharton Interactive Media pres. (4/27) on Obama Campaign?
9:00 AM Apr 10th

 davidbullock I could send more details in e-mail, but it's second-year Wharton MBA's, the class is: Monetizing Interactive Media, u would be our surprise
9:03 AM Apr 10th

David replies back that he can participate in our final presentation via a Skype call, but due to Twitter's 140 character limit, the date wasn't obvious in Lee's tweet, so David thinks the call is happening immediately:

 davidbullock Sure that would be great... I have another call @ 8:30am
9:05 AM Apr 10th

Brent Leary and David Bullock

davidbullock david@davidbullock.net

9:06 AM Apr 10th

Lee is simultaneously e-mailing David more details about the call and project while he is Tweeting back:

davidbullock I am emailing you the details right now. The call would be on April 27th at 3:15 p.m. or so. Only a 5 to 10 minute committment for you.

9:10 AM Apr 10th

David responds to the e-mail and Tweet regarding the proposed call, and provides Lee with his phone number. Five minutes later they were on the phone discussing the proposed call and other opportunities.

Exhibit 5: Timeline of Major New Media initiatives for Obama Campaign

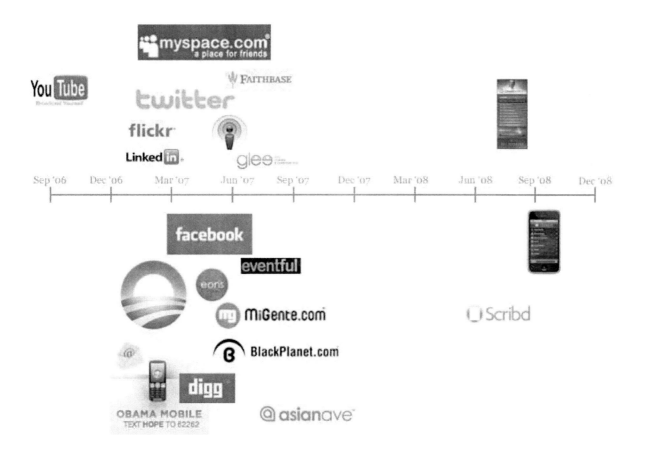

Exhibit 6: Timeline of Major New Media initiatives for Obama Campaign

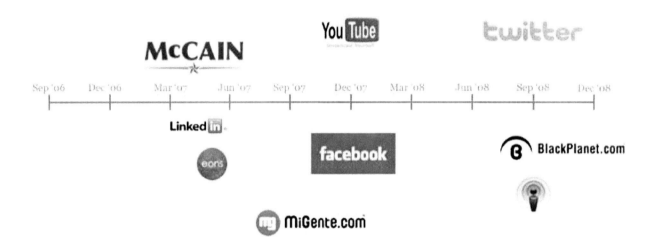

Exhibit 7: Number of tweets sent by the Obama Campaign

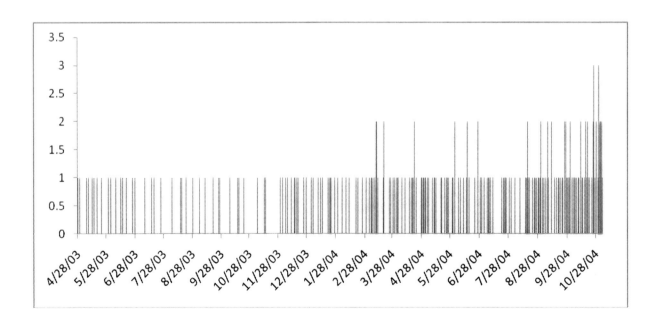

Library of Links

Brent Leary's Social CRM Blog	http://www.brentleary.com/
David Bullock - Reduce Costs, Increase Sales, Grow Profits	http://www.davidbullock.com/
50 Most Powerful and Influential Men in Social Media	http://immediateinfluenceblog.com/50-most-powerful-and-influential-men-in-social-media/
Barack 2.0 Webinar - Part 1	http://barack20.com/downloads/Video 1
Barack 2.0 Webinar - Part 2	http://barack20.com/downloads/Video 2
Barack 2.0 Webinar - Enhanced Transcript And Resource Guide	http://barack20.com/downloads/Transcript1_Barack20_Webinar_1
Black Enterprise Entrepreneurs Conference	http://ec.blackenterprise.com/bootcamps/
Brent Leary's Black Enterprise Presentation	http://video.blackenterprise.com/services/link/ bcpid1610679430/bclid1600116750/bctid1607329044
David Bullock's Black Enterprise Presentation	http://video.blackenterprise.com/services/link/ bcpid1610679430/bclid1600116750/bctid1607338040
MSNBC Article - $300 Million In Contributions	http://www.msnbc.msn.com/id/25715558/
Blogger: Create Your Free Blog	http://blogger.com/start
Blogging Software, Business Blogs & Blog Services at TypePad.com	http://www.typepad.com/
WordPress.com >> Get a Free Blog Here	http://wordpress.com/ or http://wordpress.org/
Barack Obama's Facebook Page	http://www.facebook.com/barackobama?ref=s
Barack Obama's YouTube Channel	http://youtube.com/user/barackobamadotcom
YouTube - Broadcast Yourself	http://www.youtube.com/
iTunes	http://www.apple.com/itunes/

Free Online Radio - Internet Talk Radio | BlogTalkRadio	http://www.blogtalkradio.com/
LinkedIn: Relationships Matter	http://www.linkedin.com/
FriendFeed	http://www.FriendFeed.com
Google	http://www.google.com
Obama Girl's YouTube Channel	http://www.youtube.com/watch?v=wKsoXHYICqU
Small Business Trends	http://www.smallbiztrends.com/
Outtwit - Use Twitter Directly From Outlook	http://www.techhit.com/OutTwit/
Microsoft Outlook	http://office.microsoft.com/en-us/outlook/default.aspx
Twitter Search	http://search.twitter.com/
JetBlue's Twitter Page	http://twitter.com/JetBlue
Consumerist JetBlue Article	http://consumerist.com/5093978/jetblue-twitter-faster-than-customer-service-rep
Jason Calacanis – Mahalo - Twenty Thousand People To His Website From Twitter	http://www.calacanis.com/2008/04/16/twitter-sending-over-20-000-people-a-month-to-mahalo-com/
Jason Calacanis – Business Technology Radio Article	http://www.businesstechnologyradio.com/recentshows/tabid/25382/bid/2486/ Mahalo-s-Jason-Calacanis-on-Human-Search-Google-and-Web-3-0.aspx
Amazon.com: Online Shopping	http://www.amazon.com
Reviews from Epinions	http://www99.epinions.com/
Hotel Reviews From People Like You	http://www.hotels.com/
ScribD	http://www.scribd.com/
SlideShare Is The Best Place To Share Powerpoint Presentations	http://www.slideshare.net/
Facebook Home Page	http://www.facebook.com/
Google Video	http://video.google.com/
blip.tv	http://blip.tv/
Barack Obama | Change We Need | Be the First to Know	http:// www.my.barackobama.com /page/s/firsttoknow
Barack Obama's Live Stream*	http://origin.barackobama.com/live/
Barack Obama's Document List At ScribD	http://www.scribd.com/barackobama

TwitterCounter Stats: How popular are you?	http://www.twittercounter.com/
Barack Obama Campaign*	http://www.my.barackobama.com/
Barack Obama | Change We Need | VP Pick*	http://my.barackobama.com/vp
Zoho CRM, On-Demand CRM Software, Customer Relationship Management	http://crm.zoho.com/
Microsoft Office Live Small Business	http://smallbusiness.officelive.com/
Jott – Turn Your Words Into Action	http://www.jott.com/
Digg – Discover The Best Of The Web	http://digg.com/
TechCrunch - Article	http://www.techcrunch.com/2008/08/13/barack-obama-overtakes-kevin-rose-on-twitter-mccain-is-nowhere-in-sight/
MiGente – Connect With a Million Latinos Today	http://www.migente.com/
Barack Obama's MiGente Page	http://www.migente.com/your_page/index.html?profile_id=5162830& profile_name=Barack_Obama&user_id =5162830&username =Barack_Obama
TechCrunch	http://www.techcrunch.com/
Impact The Text Message Announcement Had On Sprint	http://www.betanews.com/article/Could_Obamas_VP_pick_have_triggered_ millions_in_SMS_traffic/1219772300
Washington Post article	http://www.washingtonpost.com/wp-dyn/content/article/2008/08/19/AR2008081903186.html
Fight The Smears	http://www.fightthesmears.com/
Small Biz Trends Article - Master of My Domain Names	http://www.smallbiztrends.com/2007/12/master-of-my-domain-names.html/
Barack Obama	http://www.barackobama.com/
Ketchum Interactive	http://www.ketchum.com/interactive
The Key Influencer	http://www.thekeyinfluencer.com/
The Key Influencer Twitter Page	http://www.twitter.com/keyinfluencer
Where YOU can share solutions and insights about today's most pressing and challenging issues.	http://www.forrealsolutions.com/

CNN.com - Breaking News, U.S., World, Weather, Entertainment & Video	http://www.cnn.com/
Fastcompany.Com - Where Ideas And People Meet | Fast Company	http://www.fastcompany.com/ - GeekSexy Blog
MySpace – A Place For Friends	http://www.myspace.com/
Ustream – Live, Interactive Broadcasting	http://www.ustream.tv/
Barack Obama's Ustream Page	http://www.ustream.tv/ObamaForAmerica
Disqus - Turn Blog Comments into a Webwide Discussion with a Powerful Comment System	http://disqus.com/
FlickR - - Photo Sharing	http://flickr.com/
Meetup - Use The Internet To Get Off The Internet	http://www.meetup.com/
Barack Obama's Meetup Page	http://barackobama.meetup.com/
Brent Leary's Inc. Magazine Article - *Going Beyond Facebook, Youtube And Twitter*	http://technology.inc.com/internet/articles/200809/leary.html
Blog World Expo – Industry-wide Conference, Tradeshow & Media Event for All New Media	http://www.blogworldexpo.com/
Dipdive	http://www.dipdive.com/
Hope.Act.Change	http://www.hopeactchange.com/
Twitter's 2008 Election Page	http://www.election.twitter.com
Technorati - Real-Time Search For User-Generated Media	http://www.technorati.com/
TiVo: Your Ultimate Source For Entertainment	http://www.tivo.com/

*All Barack Obama 2008 Campaign Offices officially closed December 19, 2008. Campaign related web references may or may not be accessible.

From the Wharton Interactive Media Initiative - Engaged, Empowered & Mobilized

[i] www.aiim.org/Infonomics/Obama-How-Web2.0-Helped-Win-Whitehouse.aspx

[ii] Barack Obama's Social Media Lessons for Business , David Bullock and Brent Leary

[iii] www.fastcompany.com/magazine/134/boy-wonder.html?page=0%2C5

[iv] All voting statistics are from: www.archives.gov/federal-register/electoral-college/

[v] http://www.skittles.com/chatter.htm

[vi] www.nytimes.com/2009/01/29/fashion/29facebook.html?_r=1&partner=rss&emc=rss

[vii] http://www.brandrepublic.com/News/874030/Facebook-blocks-Burger-Kings-ditch-10-friends-app/

[viii] John Deighton and Leora Kornfeld, HBS Case titled: "Obama versus Clinton: The You Tube Primary"

[ix] Barack Obama's Social Media Lessons for Business, by David Bullock and Brent Leary

[x] Barack Obama's Social Media Lessons for Business, by David Bullock and Brent Leary

[xi] en.wikipedia.org/wiki/Gross_Rating_Point

[xii] John Deighton and Leora Kornfeld, HBS Case titled: "Obama versus Clinton: The You Tube Primary"

[xiii] www.techcrunch.com/2008/04/11/stats-obama-still-winning-on-the-web/

[xiv] As of 4/22/09

[xv] www.youtube.com/barackobamadotcom

[xvi] www.dictionary.com

[xvii] D. Bullock & B. Leary discuss the cost efficiency of utilizing YouTube to recycle existing content and showcase original content

[xviii] www.youtube.com/watch?v=RsWpvkLCvu4&feature=channel_page

[xix] This idea was discussed by Brent Leary and David Bullock in Barack 2.0

[xx] www.youbama.com, their slogan is "The Citizen Generated Campaign"

[xxi] www.youbama.com/about/

[xxii] www.youbama.com/about

[xxiii] www.aiim.org/Infonomics/Obama-How-Web2.0-Helped-Win-Whitehouse.aspx

[xxiv] www.techcrunch.com/2008/08/26/study-blogs-love-obama-news-sites-love-mccain-but-mccain-is-catching-up-by-going-negative/

[xxv] www.slate.com/id/2203146/pagenum/all/#p2

[xxvi] www.slate.com/id/2203146/pagenum/all/#p2

[xxvii] www.slate.com/id/2203146/pagenum/all/#p2

[xxviii] www.slate.com/id/2203146/pagenum/all/#p2

[xxix] www.newvotersproject.org/uploads/vR/2v/vR2vTV3whpkhL5XVBlkBrQ/Youth-Vote-and-Text-Messaging.pdf

[xxx] www.newvotersproject.org/text-messaging

[xxxi] www.slate.com/id/2203146/pagenum/all/#p2

[xxxii] Obama versus Clinton: The YouTube Primary, John Deighton, Leora Kornfeld,

[xxxiii] www.technologyreview.com/printer_friendly_article.aspx?id=21222&channel=web&section=

[xxxiv] www.aiim.org/Infonomics/Obama-How-Web2.0-Helped-Win-Whitehouse.aspx

[xxxv] www.aiim.org/Infonomics/Obama-How-Web2.0-Helped-Win-Whitehouse.aspx

[xxxvi] Numbers from March 2009

[xxxvii] Numbers from March 2009

[xxxviii] www.technologyreview.com/printer_friendly_article.aspx?id=21222&channel=web&section=

[xxxix] www.twittercounter.com

[xl] my.barackobama.com/page/community/post/external_organizing/gG5F3T

[xli] my.barackobama.com/page/community/post/external_organizing/gGxjBN

[xlii] bits.blogs.nytimes.com/2008/10/02/its-obama-on-the-iphone

[xliii] www.aiim.org/Infonomics/Obama-How-Web2.0-Helped-Win-Whitehouse.aspx

xliv Social Networking and Online Videos Take Off: The Internet's Broader Role in Campaign 2008, The Pew Research Center. January 11, 2009.

xlv www.fastcompany.com/magazine/134/boy-wonder.html

xlvi www.fastcompany.com/magazine/134/boy-wonder.html?page=0%2C3

xlvii Times online: Barack Obama is master of the new Facebook politics by Andrew Sullivan, May 25, 2008

xlviii www.fastcompany.com/magazine/134/boy-wonder.html?page=0%2C3

xlix www.fastcompany.com/magazine/134/boy-wonder.html?page=0%2C4

l www.quantcast.com/profile/traffic-compare?domain0=barackobama.com&domain1=johnmccain.com&domain2=hillaryclinton.com&domain3=&domain4=&relative=Y

li Campaign Website Traffic Comparison, January 2008 (3-month rolling average). Compete.com, furnished by David Bullock

lii www.alexa.com/siteinfo/barackobama.com

liii www.alexa.com/siteinfo/barackobama.com

liv siteanalytics.compete.com/barackobama.com+johnmccain.com+hillaryclinton.com/

lv siteanalytics.compete.com/barackobama.com+johnmccain.com/?metric=uv

lvi www.quantcast.com/barackobama.com/traffic

lvii www.quantcast.com/docs/display/info/Glossary

lviii www.quantcast.com/barackobama.com

lix www.quantcast.com/johnmccain.com

lx www.quantcast.com/hillaryclinton.com

lxi Pew Internet and American Life Project: The Internet and the 2008 Election

lxii www.fastcompany.com/magazine/134/boy-wonder.html

lxiii www.aiim.org/Infonomics/Obama-How-Web2.0-Helped-Win-Whitehouse.aspx

lxiv www.fastcompany.com/magazine/134/boy-wonder.html?page=0%2C4

lxv www.opensecrets.org/pres08/weekly.php?type=Qtrs&cand1=N00009638&cand2=N00006424&cycle=2008

lxvi www.opensecrets.org/pres08/totals.php?cycle=2008

lxvii Times online: Barack Obama is master of the new Facebook politics by Andrew Sullivan, May 25, 2008

lxviii www.opensecrets.org/pres08/summary.php?cycle=2008&cid=N00009638

lxix Pew Internet and American Life Project: The Internet and the 2008 Election

lxx www.opensecrets.org/pres08/donordems.php?sortby=N

lxxi Times online: Barack Obama is master of the new Facebook politics by Andrew Sullivan, May 25, 2008

LaVergne, TN USA
18 September 2009
158380LV00001B/11/P